Organized for Life!

Your Ultimate Step-By-Step Guide
For Getting You Organized
So You Stay Organized

By Dana Rayburn

Published by:

Dana Rayburn

PO Box 1724

Phoenix, OR 97524

(503) 385-9772

ISBN# 978-0-9895154-0-5

On the Internet:

http://www.LivingtheOrganizedLife.com/

dana@livingtheorganizedlife.com

About the Author

Dana Rayburn coaches high-functioning business owners and professionals with Attention Deficit Disorder to boost productivity, grow profits, and discover a more effortless life.

Dana sees ADHD as a gift that makes life more exciting and rewarding than it would otherwise be. She helps her clients learn to use their ADHD to their advantage and to set themselves up for success.

A professional coach since 1998, Dana came to coaching after eight years as a professional organizer teaching practical ways to manage paper, stuff, space, and time to businesses and individuals. Prior to that, she was business systems analyst for Hughes Aircraft Company in Los Angeles.

A magna cum laude graduate of California State University, Dominguez Hills with a degree in business administration, Dana is a graduate of the Optimal Functioning Institute and Coach U.

Dana and her family live in the beautiful Rogue River Valley in Southern Oregon. In her spare time, she enjoys hiking, gardening, Nordic skiing, reading, and chauffeuring her daughter about town.

Read Dana's articles about living successfully with ADHD and sign up for her popular monthly newsletter, ADDed Success, at www.danarayburn.com.

ACKNOWLEDGEMENTS

My deepest thanks goes to my husband Scott and my aunt Pat Lang for their editing skills and loving support during the years it took me to write this book. Also, to my coach and idea midwife, Laura Linn-Blum. I couldn't have written 'Organized for Life' without you.

In addition, many people have contributed essential information to my knowledge about getting organized. Special thanks go to my family and all the clients I've helped organize over the years.

Finally, the following three books made a huge difference in helping me learn to be an organized person. I am eternally grateful for the authors' wisdom and encouragement.

Sandra Felton, *Messies Manual* – _The Procrastinators Guide to Good Housekeeping_, (Fleming H, Revell Co., 1983).

Pam Young and Peggy Jones, _Sidetracked Home Executives – From Pigpen to Paradise_, 2nd. ed. (Binford & Mort, 1980).

Marla Cilley – The FlyLady, _Sink Reflections – FlyLady's Baby Step Guide to Overcoming CHAOS_, (FlyLady Press, Inc., 2002).

Contents

Welcome to Organized for Life

Introduction

It's the morning after entertaining friends for dinner. I'm sitting in my living room relaxed and content. Everything is sparkling clean. The house looks great.

As I admire my shiny home, I remember other mornings after other parties...when the house looked great, but I was far from relaxed and anything but content; the many times I still was frazzled and exhausted from getting the house decent enough for friends and family to enter. Entertaining wasn't fun then. But now it is.

I'm Dana Rayburn and I was born disorganized. From the time I could walk until I was 28 years old, I was the poster child for disorganized living.

When I lived with my parents, my bedroom was a cluttered disaster area; toys, books, and dirty clothes ruled and my homework was rarely done.

When I had my own apartment, my bills were paid late and closets were crammed with all manner of junk. Have you ever worn wet pantyhose because you hadn't done the laundry and had to wash a pair right before leaving for work? YUCK! I used to do it all the time.

When I got married I took my messy ways with me. My poor husband had no idea what he was getting into because by then I was a secret messy.

When people visited my home or office, the surfaces looked pretty good but piles and clutter lurked below. I looked pulled together, but it was all a façade. I was the same disorganized person as always, only I worked really, really hard to hide the fact.

About a year into my marriage three things happened that prompted me to change. First, I developed a serious dust allergy. Merely being in my home would send me into sneezing fits. Dust is a cleaning issue, but when a home is drowning in clutter, dusting is hard to do. Second, my darling husband no longer found my messy ways adorable. He's a tidy kind of guy and looking into the future I saw the sad toll my mess would take on our marriage. Third, I was tired of the lies and stress it took to hide my messy ways. I value honesty and easy living and my secret disorganization violated values daily.

I decided I simply had to make changes in my life and behavior. I took a class, read lots of books, and studied how organized people lived. Three years and three large garage sales later, I had changed my messy ways.

It's been a transformation on so many levels, a journey from being messy-to-the-max to organized-for-life. And it's been one of the most rewarding accomplishments of my life.

Along with rehabilitating my self-image and creating a new career out of what I learned, I've discovered many things:

- Life is easier when you're organized. Your days flow more easily. Fewer hassles pop up. You're more calm and relaxed.

- You have more time for fun when you aren't constantly searching for things.

- You are more creative when you aren't stressed from juggling to keep everything together.

- You have better relationships when you're organized. People trust you will do what you say you'll do and be where you say you'll be.
- You experience less stress and conflict at home over messes and problems.

But here's the most important lesson, the one I'm most eager to share with you:

Changing from a messy person to being organized for life involves much more than simply learning lots of tips and tricks. Becoming and staying organized for life truly happens only when you learn to think and act like an organized person.

I've written this book because people tell me they are inspired and encouraged by my own story. They want to learn more about how a person who was born messy could learn to get organized and stay organized.

Here's what I tell them:

My story is a simple one. And I believe that if I tell you my story and share my discoveries, you can learn, too. You can use my experiences and knowledge to organize your world, and get organized so you stay organized. Because staying organized is what it's all about.

Not too long ago I received this note from a woman: "I don't need to know *how* to get organized. I've gotten organized over and over again. What I need to know is how to *stay* organized!"

What I want for her, and for you, is to experience transformation as I've experienced it.

I want you to be relaxed and competent and comfortable with

your world and how it runs.

I want you to feel the surprised glow of pride the first time someone tells you how wonderfully organized you are.

I want you to be able to have people over to your home on the spur of the moment without an attack of panic or guilt.

I want you to be free for creativity and fun.

How to Use This Book

Organized for Life! is a step-by-step guide for teaching you how to get organized so you can stay organized. One step leads to the next. Skipping a step won't do you any favors. It merely makes it harder to succeed. So please, please, PLEASE, start at the beginning and work your way through.

In the first six chapters you'll build your foundation for getting organized so you stay organized. These are **important steps you must not skip!** However, I do realize you may be itching to see physical signs of progress. That's why I've included some opportunities for early action. You'll find them under the heading "If You've Gotta Do Something" and they'll give you a quick organizing chore to do.

You won't find page after page devoted to organizing tips and tricks for each room of your home and office in *Organized for Life!* That's not my purpose. I've found most people don't need more tips. They need to know how to get organized so they stay organized. Many other good books dedicated to organizing tips are available. One of my favorites is *Organizing for Dummies* by Eileen Roth and Elizabeth Miles.

Part One

Getting
Organized for
Life

CHAPTER 1

the organized for life difference

Being disorganized is a drag. It increases your stress level, taxes your relationships, and damages your self-esteem. It also wastes money and time.

When you're disorganized:

- You can't find what you need when you need it or remember what to do when you need to do it.
- Your bills are paid late.
- You can't remember the last time you balanced your checkbook.
- Your children have to turn their underwear inside out because they can't find a clean pair to wear.
- You panic at the thought of visitors dropping by your house unexpectedly and seeing the clutter.
- Your spouse or partner is disgusted by—and critical of— your clutter and sloppy habits.

- You are disgusted by—and critical of—your clutter and sloppy habits.

Life doesn't have to be that hard! Say it to yourself, slowly: **Life doesn't have to be that hard.**

Neither does change. When you approach getting organized in a practical way with the focus on making it easy and what's important, you'll find it almost effortless to be organized.

WHY MOST ORGANIZING BOOKS DON'T HELP

There are some excellent books out there about organizing. Yet most books about being organized have a common problem: their authors were born organized. These are people who find it naturally easy to put things away and clear clutter. Another problem is the books are full of tips and tricks for getting organized, but don't take the critical next step of walking you through the process.

I promise you this book is different. Remember, I was born messy and though I've changed, I know from hard, personal experience that much of the usual advice about getting organized just doesn't work for messy people. And it's not because messy people don't try.

Most messy people are disorganized not because they are lazy. They are disorganized because they don't know any other way to be, and the ways they are told to be organized are too hard and too overwhelming.

To transform yourself into an organized person you must learn to think and act like an organized person. Then, you need to discover easy ways to outsmart the mess, and keep outsmarting it on a continuing basis.

WHY YOU SHOULD LISTEN TO ME

I'm a reformed messy person. The first 28 years of my life were lived in a constant battle of disorganization, a battle I usually lost. It was stressful and confusing. I wasted a lot of time, a lot of money, and consumed a lot of energy feeling guilty and thinking of excuses to hide what I had or hadn't done.

When I was newly married, I reached my messiness breaking point; I could no longer expect my parents to cover for me.

I was no longer a young single woman, enjoying a free-spirit life, where no one cared how tidy my apartment was.

I had a husband I adored and after about a year of marriage, I could see a future of pain and conflict unless I mended my messy ways. Most of all, I was just plain tired of the stress and hassle of being disorganized.

It so happens I have a gift for being able to look at a task and figure out how to make it easier. When I set my mind to something, I can watch how other people do things and adjust it to work for me.

So when I decided I didn't want to be a mess any longer, I set my mind to figuring out how to be organized. I attended classes and read organizing books.

I secretly studied how the naturally organized people in my life did things. And I experimented with different techniques and methods until gradually, in about three years, the clutter was gone and I was living an organized enough life.

After a few years, my husband and I moved to a rural area where my job skills weren't needed, and I was looking for work. A woman asked me if I could help her get organized and I said sure. That started my eight-year stint as a professional organizer, giving workshops and teaching people in their businesses and homes the same tricks and techniques I taught myself for how to get organized to stay organized.

In 2000, I completed training to become a life coach to help adults live more easily with Attention Deficit Hyperactivity Disorder (ADHD). Disorganization plagues people with ADHD and daily I help my clients build organizing systems and create clarity from chaos.

Why should you listen to me? I've been where you are. I dug myself out of a messy place, and I've built a business around helping people who desire a more organized life dig out as well.

WHAT IS EFFORTLESS ORGANIZING?

I've found that most messy people think being organized means spending hours each day tending to their home and possessions. They think things will rarely be out of place and even tiny messes won't be tolerated. They fear they will be required to do things far in advance.

Let's be clear about expectations – in my view, being organized is merely a tool for making life more simple and relaxing.

This isn't about your house being so neat it looks like no one lives there. I don't want you to be so compulsively tidy that your family and friends don't want to be with you. And I surely do not intend for you to spend all your free time straightening and cleaning!

You likely know people who are compulsively tidy, and that's fine for them. These are people who were born organized! Frankly, it sounds like too much work to me! For those of us who were born messy, that lifestyle isn't even an option.

What is an option – what I emphasize – is what I call Effortless

Organizing. The premise is simple: **staying organized must be simple and quick or it just won't happen.**

Effortless Organizing is a casual, pretty-organized-most-of-the-time approach to life. Your focus is on the quickest and easiest ways you can create a comfortable home you and your family like to be in and are proud to bring your friends into.

One of the biggest benefits of this approach is all the newly found free time you'll have.

You know you're <u>Effortlessly</u> Organized when:

- You can usually find what you need quickly without panic or searching.

- You can tidy up any clutter quickly because you know where everything belongs and the things you use the most are easiest to put away. Small piles may accumulate, but don't hang around long before being cleared away.

- You don't have to remember what you need to do and when you need to do it. Instead you use a system of clear reminders so you usually get things done on time without undue panic.

- You take a 'this is good enough' approach to managing your home and stuff. You might not want *House Beautiful* magazine to drop in unexpected, but your friends and neighbors can without causing you embarrassment.

- You spend a few minutes most days tending to your home knowing that it's the small, steady steps that make the most difference.

- You have oodles of time to do other things. Even if you have a full-time job outside your home, you can have personal playtime and an Effortlessly Organized home at the same time.

Here's the most exciting part: When you're Effortlessly Organized you don't just get organized, you stay organized for the rest of your life! Because things are easy to do and you've created friendly routines and simple habits to keep you on track.

The Hidden Costs of Disorganization

You know how expensive disorganization is, right? Some of the costs are obvious—like late fees, wasted time and lost opportunities. But there are hidden costs of disorganization, too. Costs that are less obvious yet add an extra whammy if you're struggling to manage an already overwhelming life.

The formula goes something like this: physical disorganization fuels emotional distress and mental chaos.

When you can't get organized it takes a toll. Each time you look at your home, your desk or your car, the piles and clutter send messages straight to your psyche.

The Four Hidden Costs of Disorganization

1. *The Cost of Confusion.*

   When your world is cluttered, life is more confusing. You won't know where to start and can't figure out what to do next. Without a starting point to grab onto, your thoughts start spinning, only making the confusion worse.

2. *The Cost of Distraction.*

   Clutter and disorganization are distracting. With a

plethora of things lying about to catch your eye, you'll get pulled off track more easily. A simpler, clearer environment makes it easier to stay focused.

3. *The Cost of Overwhelm.*

    As disorganization builds, it becomes harder and harder for the brain to focus. Simply looking at all the decisions you need to make and actions you need to take can flip your mental switch into overwhelm. When you get overwhelmed, any task becomes nearly impossible to make progress on.

4. *The Cost of Negative Self-Talk.*

    As a former ADD coaching client, Sean, so eloquently put it, "When I look at the piles and the clutter it reinforces my belief that I'm a failure. That I have no hope of ever getting a handle on managing my ADHD. Everywhere I look I see what a loser I am."

These emotional costs can block what needs to be done to get organized and to handle the problem. It's a catch-22. Many adults tend to make light of the clutter. But clutter takes us into dark places.

Clutter increases the challenge of living more successfully with Attention Deficit. The hidden costs of disorganization are nothing to laugh about.

Magic Wand Not Included

Becoming Effortlessly Organized doesn't happen overnight. You cannot do in a weekend.

Getting organized so you can stay organized is a process of adopting new habits, learning new skills, and developing self-awareness. It's an ebb and flow of little steps forward and backward; sometimes you will fail and let yourself down. But gradually, day-by-day, week-by-week, and year-by-year you'll get stronger and better at it.

That's why from the start I want you to approach being organized as a long-term project of gradual improvement. As you take little steps forward to your goal, you'll discover payoffs that ripple through all areas of your life. You will find success!

CHAPTER 1 SUMMARY

KEY POINTS TO REMEMBER ABOUT GETTING ORGANIZED FOR LIFE

- **Effortless Organizing** is a casual, pretty-organized-most-of-the-time approach to life where you focus on the quickest and easiest ways you can create a tidy, comfortable home for you and your family.

- **Becoming Effortlessly Organized** isn't a quick fix; it's a long-term project of gradual improvement where you learn to get organized so you stay organized.

Chapter 2

Background Stuff You Need to Know

Before we start, I'd like to clarify a couple of things for you. Things that will increase your understanding and perspective about what we're up to.

The Three Organizing Personalities

To become organized for life you must alter your habits and viewpoint to be more like those of an organized person. Perhaps an explanation of the three organizing personalities will help.

There are three basic types of people when it comes to organizing: those who are naturally organized those who are naturally messy, and those who are reformed messy people.

Naturally Organized People

Naturally organized people find it second nature to sort and keep track of things. Their homes and offices are always neat. Clutter is kept to a minimum. They send birthday cards on time. Their kid's fingernails are clean and trimmed. Their projects are on schedule. Everything in their Day Planner is filed and recorded under the proper tab.

My sister is naturally organized. When we were kids her bedroom was always neat. She can pull off a massive project calmly with all the details attended to and still manage to send a birthday gift so it arrives on time.

My daughter is naturally organized. From the start she liked to have things just so. That's not to say that her room isn't sometimes a disaster area. But when push comes to shove, she likes things to be tidy. I must admit it's a tad unnerving when your six-year old picks up after you!

Some people can be too organized. It's a compulsion. They can't relax. They must control. They are never satisfied because nothing they do is good enough.

In high school, my best friend's mom was like that. She drove her family crazy with her need to be organized. Once, when their house was burgled, my friend's mom wiped away all the bad-guy's muddy footprints before the police came so they wouldn't think her a slob.

Naturally Messy People

The next organizing personality I call Naturally Messy People. Naturally Messy People leave clutter and chaos in their wake.

They can't relax because they are too busy looking for their keys. They're afraid someone will drop by before they've had time to shove all the piles in the guest room and bolt the door. Left to their own devices, they can't be bothered to put things away, close cupboards, or remember to do things.

They don't know how to think like an organized person. They don't know how to set up their home or office to make life easier so, naturally, the mess gets worse.

I was born a naturally messy person. Let me tell you about one of my shining moments of shame. It happened many years ago, the day a good friend called to tell me she was in the neighborhood and about to drop by my apartment for a visit. Caught off-guard, I couldn't think up an excuse for why she couldn't come over. So I hung up the phone and dashed around scooping up piles to stash in my favorite hiding place: the empty dishwasher. Soon my friend arrived and commented she didn't know how I kept my apartment so tidy! I smiled sweetly on the outside but inside I felt about two inches tall. I was a fraud.

Many messy people practice 'yo-yo organizing'. They occasionally go on clearing clutter and tidying binges only to find the mess quickly returns.

Problems really arise when someone is so messy she or he can't throw anything away without suffering an anxiety attack. These are the folks you read about whose house is condemned as a fire danger from the stacks of newspapers.

Compulsive hoarding is a psychological disorder that results in wall-to-wall, floor-to-ceiling stockpiling of clutter that interferes with daily living. Though this book may help a compulsive hoarder learn basic organizational skills, often therapy and medications are needed to change the hoarding behavior.

REFORMED MESSIES

My third organizing personality is Reformed Messies. Reformed Messies are people who are naturally messy but with the right approach and attitude they have learned to be organized.

I'm a reformed messy.

Actually, I'm a reformed messy on a mission. A mission to turn you into a reformed messy, too!

The best way I know of becoming a reformed messy is learning the things I'll teach you in this book. Actually, do more than learn them. Make them an integral part of your life!

Let me tell you about another reformed messy: Joe, 49, had recently gotten divorced when he called for organizing help. He'd gotten married fresh out of college to a woman who was naturally organized. For 26 years she ran their house with ease.

When they divorced, Joe found himself living on his own for the first time in his life. He didn't have a clue about how to be organized. The clutter had gotten so bad that Joe was afraid he'd have to get married again just to have someone organize him!

Thankfully, Joe called me instead of a dating service. I worked with Joe for 14 months teaching how to be a reformed messy. An excellent student, he learned the ins and outs of being organized; habits such as closing drawers and skills such as where to keep things.

And now? Joe is getting married again. Not because he needs a housekeeper but because he's in love with a great woman!

WHAT ABOUT YOUR FAMILY?

Before you read any further, let's examine a concern of many people determined to get Organized for Life: What about your family and their impact on your organizing efforts?

(By the way, when I refer to your family, I'm referring to the people who share your home or wherever you are trying to organize. Whether it's your spouse, children, partner, roommate, or live-in nanny, if you share your space with them we'll call them your family.)

First we'll talk about something you need to be aware of regarding organizing and your family; then I'll give you some ideas for how to help them to help you become Organized for Life. Finally, we'll talk about what to do about uncooperative family members.

Be Aware

You can't organize another person if that person doesn't want to be organized.

I'll say it again: **You can't organize another person**.

Getting Organized for Life is a project requiring personal focus and determination to change. You can't force others to consistently clear their clutter and sort through their piles. Unless they want to learn for themselves how to become organized and form the necessary new habits, they will continue to be messy.

So if you live with others who are messy, your challenge becomes how to keep their messiness from stopping your own efforts to live an organized life.

Some people are lucky to have a spouse or partner who is naturally organized and children who jump in and want to put their things away. Though this is what I wish for you, please realize it rarely happens that way. It's more likely you'll be the lone organizing ship in a sea of clutter bugs. Or, perhaps your spouse will be helpful but the kids will rebel.

Does that mean you just give up and put up with clutter in your house? Not at all!

You just have to approach organizing as though it's your very own project – which it is. You graciously accept that you are the organizing force in your household and do the best you can. You don't become a martyr or shrew. You don't become a resentful nag.

You lovingly take responsibility for your decisions and actions and do what you can do. And, you don't give up no matter how hard your family makes it!

Fill Them In

You and your family are interconnected. Your behaviors and habits are formed around one another. When one person changes, the impact ripples onto all.

Let your family know you're intent on getting organized so they're prepared for things to change. Reassure them you won't start wildly throwing their things away. Tell them you'll need their support and your being organized will help all of you have a nicer place to live.

Find Out What They Need

When you are changing a routine or storage space that impacts your family get their input first. Make sure what you're up to will work for them. There may be a good reason you don't know about why they do what they do. Ask for their ideas. Work out compromises when necessary.

Let Them Know What You Need

When a family member's actions get on your nerves, avoid playing the blame game. Instead, key into the specific details of what bothers you. Then talk to the person and tell him or her exactly what you need instead. Be open to consider their needs. As we discussed in the above paragraph, they may do what they do for valid reasons you aren't aware of.

For example, perhaps they think reminding you often that you're getting organized helps you, but you'd rather they say nothing and play it low key. Tell them.

Become aware of what you need and calmly let them know. Don't make the common mistake of putting up with something until you get so angry you lose your temper.

Set it Up Right

How you set up your organizing and storage systems is crucial to encouraging your family to play along.

If you find your family is able to make such a large mess that all your hard organizing work is undone in a few minutes, that's a sign you're merely surface organizing – making things tidy without following the rules and guidelines I'll give you throughout this book. Believe me, if the correct organizing structure exists. You can clean up seemingly huge messes in a matter of minutes.

Make it Easy

Design your organizing and storage systems so it's easy for your family to find things and put things away. Hopefully, if it's easy enough to do, they will.

Give them easy to use places to keep their stuff: a basket on the dresser for your husband to empty his pockets into instead of tossing it all on the table; a hook by the back door to hang your son's backpack instead of dropping it in the entry hall (don't worry, pages of this book are dedicated to making it easy to find things and put them away).

Teach Them How

You can't expect the people you live with to magically know where things go, so you'll have to train them. You need to patiently explain it to them – likely more than once.

When you're dealing with children, be sure to give them specific instructions. You'll have more success with, "pick up the dirty clothes off your floor and put them in the laundry hamper," than a general, "go clean your room".

Set Ground Rules

Make a rule or two. Some families have great success allowing the kids to have only one toy out at a time (this doesn't work in our house). Whatever rules you decide, I suggest you work them out with your family. No sense coming up with rules no one will even try to follow!

The rule for my family is this: you can make a mess in your own area but you need to clean up your stuff in the rest of the house. It's sort of a private space versus public space thing. My messy areas are my kitchen junk drawer and my office. Scott's messy areas are his office, the workbench, and one corner of the garage. Aja's messy area is her bedroom. Now, none of these areas are what you would look at and call a disaster, but they can get a bit out of control without upsetting anyone else in the family.

Make Clear Consequences

Along with rules you need to make clear consequences so people know what happens if they break the rules.

You've got lots of options here. It likely will depend what the mess is and who makes it. Everyone makes mistakes and little kids are little kids. For instance, our daughter knows that if she's asked repeatedly to put something away and she doesn't, I'll likely give it to charity. On the other hand, my husband is pretty reliable about not leaving things lying around, so when it happens I chalk it up to an oversight and just put it away for him.

You also can forge treaties. One former organizing client, Jerry, had a paper packrat for a wife who'd let papers pile up in the kitchen and dining room. When Jerry explained he was learning to organize the house, they worked out a deal. Here's how it worked: Jerry would collect any papers his wife left lying about and neatly pile them on her desk. He had her permission to sort and toss any piles that started to ooze from her desk onto the floor.

Last Resort – If Someone Won't Cooperate

All right, these are drastic measures. But if someone truly won't cooperate, and you've tried the ideas above, and you've tried to reason with them, then you'll have to do what you must do — especially if this person's clutter presents a choice of you achieving your organized existence or not.

Here's how one client, Tory, handles the chaos and clutter caused by her uncooperative husband. She has repeatedly asked him for his help and has made it easy for him to put stuff away, but for whatever reason, he just won't. Blessed with separate his and hers walk-in closets, Tory collects her husband's mess from around the house, dumps it in his closet and shuts the door. Tory admits her husband's closet looks as though it has been ransacked. But the rest of the house is tidy and Tory is happy. She figures if he really cared, he'd clean it up.

I read of one couple who would stash their teenage son's clutter in a box and if he didn't put his stuff away in a week they'd get rid of it for him.

If you've a family member who is so messy you can't keep up, it may be an issue of conscious or unconscious sabotage, which may be a symptom of other problems. You need to decide if you want to put up with it, get counseling, or make some changes, no matter how difficult or uncomfortable.

Remember, It's For You!

Remember, you are doing this for you! Your family may benefit, but you are the one who will gain the most by becoming organized for life. You're the one who will harvest the peace and calm and good feelings of a tidy welcoming home. Stay positive. Set good examples and know you're doing it for you.

Chapter 2 Summary

Key Points to Remember About the Background Stuff You Need to Know

- The **Three Organizing Personalities** are:
  - **Naturally Organized People** – born organized, they find it easy to stay that way. We can learn a lot from these folks!
  - **Naturally Messy People** – born to cause clutter and chaos.
  - **Reformed Messies** – People who were born messy but have learned to be organized. This is your goal!
- **Help your family** to help you by:
  - Filling them in on your organizing project.
  - Finding out their needs and telling them yours.
  - Making it easy for them to find things and put them away. And teaching them how to use your new organizing systems.
  - Setting ground rules and making clear consequences.

Part Two

Getting Started and Digging Out

Chapter 3

Step One: Setting Yourself Up for Success

Organizing Failure Formula

I truly want you to become organized for life. That's why I want you to know there are numerous ways you can fail:

- You can blame your disorganization on other people. Your husband, your mother, your kids, or your dog.

- You can blame your disorganization on your health. Your ADHD, your depression, your weight, or your lack of energy.

- You can blame it on your life. You work too hard. Or, my all-time favorite, you're too busy.

You've likely heard the saying, "Keep doing what you're doing and you'll keep getting what you've got." Everyone has challenges. Take a stand and make what you want a priority. Retrain the people in your life. Get treatment for your health problems.

I realize I risk sounding callous and uncaring here. Believe me, I'm not. I'm just not going to stand by and watch you play the blame game and make excuses.

If you want to change your life and get organized, I'm beside you all the way. If you want to stay in your messy existence, at least be honest with yourself about it.

ORGANIZING SUCCESS FORMULA

You can succeed at getting organized, but you will need to embrace these five components of my Organizing Success Formula to reach your goal:

1. Accept your Disorganization
2. Commit to Changing
3. Intend to be Organized
4. Visualize Neat
5. Retrain your brain

Let's cover the Organizing Success Formula in detail, shall we?

1. ACCEPT YOUR DISORGANIZATION

Do you remember the classic TV show *Bewitched*? I adored that show when I was a kid. I would stand in my bedroom door and wiggle my nose hoping beyond hope my bedroom would magically become clean. I compelled the piles to disappear so my mom would let me go out and play.

Well, it never worked. Are you surprised? Yet for years I waited for some magical outside force to come along and clear up the mess for me. **It wasn't until I accepted that it was *my* problem and I had to deal with it that I began to change.**

Yes, many of us have families who add to the mess. Believe me,

I'm very aware of the havoc little kids, big kids, and messy spouses or partners can cause.

But realistically, what's your choice? You can wallow in the community mess frustrated and ashamed, or you can decide to do the best you can to change the only one you can change: YOU.

And I promise, when you embrace an attitude of acceptance your circumstances will improve. It may take a while, but your family will come around. With your example and gentle guidance they, too, will learn to do better.

2. COMMIT TO CHANGING

Let's be clear: I want this book to do more than simply teach you some organizing tips.

I want you to experience the same organization transformation I've experienced. I want you to wake up some bright, sunny morning and realize you aren't messy any more. I want you to suddenly realize you are an organized person.

That's why I am challenging you right now, before you read any further, to make a commitment. I hope this challenge inspires you to achieve far more than you ever thought possible.

I want you to make the commitment to rise above all the negative junk that's in your head.

I want you to make the commitment to ignore all those people in your family and life who put you down for being messy.

IGNORE THEM!

I want you to make the commitment to yourself right now that you are going to step onto the path to being Organized for Life. A journey of continuous improvement where every week from now on, you see your home and your office become more organized.

After all, who ever thought a total slob like me could transform into an organized person! Plus make my living by helping other people become organized! I never did. My family never did. It just kind of happened. I worked at it a tiny bit at a time. Made gradual improvements. Enjoyed the ups and worked through the downs. Ignored the negative comments. And one day I woke up and looked around and realized I was a different person….a person who was organized!

I want more for you than the accidental transformation I experienced. I want you to know now, up front, before you take one more step, that it's possible. I want you to know you can do it!

A lot of what you're dealing with is a psychological barrier. You may want to live an organized life, but deep in your gut you believe you're a messy person, a total slob. You don't think it's possible.

That's why I'm challenging you to aim to become someone much greater than you already are. I want you to aim for more than a clear dining room table or a garage with enough open space to park your car.

I challenge you to make a commitment to transform into an organized person!

Ready? Take the Commitment Pledge!

Raise your right hand and repeat the following. Better yet, write it out and sign it:

I, (say your name), commit to doing the best I can to become an organized person. I don't expect to be perfect, I just commit to doing my best. I will control only what I can control – ME! I will ignore the negative comments of others and my own negative thoughts. I commit to celebrating my successes and getting back on track should I fall off my path.

Sign Your Name

Date

3. INTEND TO BE ORGANIZED

A crucial step in getting organized for life is getting clear about how you want you and your world to be. You must set an intention. It must be an intention you think about often. An intention to keep you moving on your path to becoming organized for life.

Many books about change and self-improvement will suggest you write out your intentions or goals. I prefer a slightly different approach.

In my experience, unless someone is incredibly focused and organized, written goals and time lines merely set the person up to fail. After all, if you were focused and organized you wouldn't have felt the need to purchase this book, would you?

Also, for someone challenged with becoming organized, a piece of paper with written goals would soon be lost amid the rest of the clutter.

Don't get me wrong, I firmly believe you must have a goal or intention to succeed. We'll just do it a bit differently than others do, that's all.

Let's set your intentions

Please do this with me right now. This is important. Don't fool yourself into thinking you'll skip this and come back and do it later. You won't. **Do it now!**

- Stop reading for a moment. Sit back, take a deep breath and let it out. Relax.

- Let's get clear on your intentions. (Okay, write your intentions out if you feel you must, but don't let it stop you if you can't find a piece of paper or a pen with ink in it. And if you do write them out, for heaven's sake, don't stress out if you lose the piece of paper!)

- Imagine how your house will look when you're organized; how you will feel, who else will benefit.

- Now, consider what you imagined to answer this question: "I will know I'm an organized person when…" Try to come up with around five things. These will be your intentions.

- Keep your answers positive. For instance, "We eat dinner on our clear, shiny dining room table," is more positive than, "I finally get off my rear and throw away the old newspapers and stacks of junk mail so we can eat in the dining room." Go for positive!!

4. VISUALIZE NEAT

Okay, you're clear about your five intentions, right? (If you're not, please go back to *Let's Set Your Intentions* directly above and follow the steps to set your intentions.)

Next you are going to visualize the end result you want to achieve. You're going to make that picture big and bright and put it right in front of you.

I call this **Visualize Neat** and find it does two things.

1. It combats the step-over-and-ignore reflex of most messy people. When you visualize neat you are more apt to notice the mess when you open your eyes.

2. Visualizing Neat also helps you more easily create your organized home. By attaching feelings to what you are visualizing, your intentions become even more powerful.

Let's give it a try:

Close your eyes right now and imagine what your organized home looks like.

Peek in the rooms and see how neat and tidy they are. Imagine how you feel when your home looks the way you dream it can.

Picture who else benefits from your tidy home. Imagine your family enjoying it.

Make your picture bigger and brighter. Give it a golden glow, if you can.

The more often you **Visualize Neat,** the better. I suggest you try for twice a day: in the morning when you awake and at night before you fall asleep. It only takes a moment.

Meg was a telephone coaching client who called because clutter was overrunning her house. Meg's dining room had become a major junk heap. The table was piled with newspapers, junk mail, unfinished projects, and things that needed to be put away. Meg wanted it cleared off.

One of the first things I had Meg do was visualize neat. Her coaching homework was to close her eyes twice a day and spend a few moments picturing a clear table with a lovely centerpiece gracing the middle. Meg was skeptical but she agreed to try it.

On our next coaching call Meg reported she'd done her homework. She grumbled how now, for the first time, she actually noticed the mess.

Ah ha! My plan was working. By our next appointment, Meg couldn't stand the mess any longer; she'd started wading through the clutter. Soon we were setting up systems to keep her table forever free from clutter!

5. RETRAIN YOUR BRAIN

What else needs to happen before you can change? (And yes, we're talking about change here.)

You must become aware. Aware of what you're doing. Aware of where you have problems. How can you become aware? The Visualizing Neat exercise we discussed above is an excellent start, and I'm about to tell you about another technique to boost your success even more.

You need to retrain your brain. If you faithfully use this technique, you'll gradually find you can do the things you intend to do. You'll clear off your desk before you leave the office for the day. You'll file those papers. You'll put the dishes away and notice the pile of laundry on the living room sofa.

Try this simple exercise:

1. Close your eyes and imagine a yellow triangle perfectly centered within a red circle.

2. Keep picturing that image for as long as you can. At which moment do other ideas, thoughts, emotions, visual images, sounds or feelings intrude?

If you're typical, and honest with yourself, you didn't make it more than three seconds.

What intruded is "your stream of consciousness."

For example, here's how it might sound if I were to describe what I intended to do at this moment (write this section) and included the interruptions from my stream of consciousness. My stream of consciousness thoughts are in parenthesis:

⊙ *I want to describe retraining the brain.*

⊙ *(It's 3:30 and Steven hasn't called for his coaching session.)*

⊙ *(I'll wait five more minutes before I call him.)*

⊙ *Do I start with the word example or …?*

⊙ *(I hope I have time to go to the gym tonight.)*

⊙ *No, that word is too complicated.*

⊙ *(My right eyebrow itches.)*

⊙ *(Oh, an email just came in. Maybe I'll look at it.)*

⊙ *No, I'll finish this section first.*

That's the sort of thing that goes on all the time. Check it out for yourself. Imagine trying to give someone else instructions that included your stream of consciousness. They'd get totally confused wouldn't they!

The problem is your unconscious hears all of your stream of consciousness. How can it possibly decipher what is important and what is unimportant?

The answer is: **NORMALLY IT CAN'T!**

It can't unless you tell it what you want it to pay attention to. You've got to put a bull's eye squarely on what you want. You've got to help your unconscious separate what is important from everything else in your stream of consciousness.

Separating Success from Failure

To Retrain Your Brain you'll use an extremely simple and powerful technique for instructing your unconscious. In fact, it's so simple you might think it's silly.

But if you try it, you'll increase your likelihood of success.

1. Starting now, and as you go through your day, pay attention to your actions.

2. When you do something that moves you closer to being

organized say to yourself, "that's a **success. I want more success!**"

3. When you do something that moves you away from being organized, say to yourself, "that's a **failure**. I don't want any of those!"

For an example, let's apply this to my morning. As I go through my morning I tell my brain what I consider to be a success and what isn't. Let's try it. This morning my intention was to dress, eat breakfast, do my morning house chores, and get to my home office early.

- I combed and fed the pets (success).

- I put away last night's dishes and quickly wiped the sink and counters (success).

- I watched a cartoon with my daughter. I spent time with her (success) but I also got off track and aimlessly stared at the TV for five minutes (failure).

- I ate a good breakfast (success) but forgot to take my vitamins (failure).

- I forgot to water the houseplants (failure).

- I showered and dressed (success).

- I finally watered the houseplants (success).

- I got to my home office 15 minutes early (success) but neglected to start a load of laundry (failure).

If you do this every day, you will soon see that the daily number of successes increase and the number of failures decrease simply because you consciously told your unconscious to focus on generating successes and reducing failures.

What you focus on is an instruction to your unconscious. If you want more success, focus on success.

You can do it. I know you can!

Chapter 3 Summary

Key Points to Remember About Setting Yourself Up for Success

- The **Organizing Failure Formula** – making excuses and blaming others for your disorganization.

- The **Organizing Success Formula**:
    - Accept your Disorganization
    - Commit to Changing
    - Intend to be Organized
    - Visualize Neat

Review Questions

1. What about your life or situation must you accept before you can become Organized for Life?

2. Have you taken the **Commitment Pledge**? If not, please go back and do so.

3. Have you clearly set your **Intention**? If not, please go back and do so.

4. Have you **Visualized Neat**? Why ever not?!?! If you haven't go back and do so!

5. From this moment on, as you go about your day, identify your successes and failures to keep you on track.

6. Visualize your organizing intention for a few moments each morning when you awaken and for a few moments each night before you go to sleep.

 CHAPTER 4

Step Two: Learning the Ground Rules

In Step One, you adjusted your attitude to keep you on the path of being organized for life as well as some tricks to make your journey easier.

I realize you are probably itching to jump right in and start clearing clutter, but I need you to hold on a bit longer.

First, you've got to do one more thing. You've got to learn the ground rules for getting organized so you stay organized for the rest of your life.

CHANGE YOUR HABITS

What is a habit, anyway? It's something you do as second-nature, an action you take without thinking. You already have lots of habits for all kinds of everyday activities.

Not surprisingly, many of your habits help keep you disorganized - habits such as ignoring the daily mail or tossing your clothes over the back of a chair.

What you need to do is develop new habits. Not just any habits, however. You must develop those golden organizing habits that will keep you organized.

I've a question for you: what one thing do you think you could do consistently to get organized so you stay organized?

- Make your bed every day?

- Put the dishes away?

- Remove the clutter from the dining room table?

These are good habits. Noble pieces in the organizing puzzle, but they won't help you reach the ultimate goal of getting organized so you stay organized.

I have a secret weapon; the missing link in many people's futile attempts to get organized: The Secret Habits of Organized People.

Tips and tricks will take you only so far. The Secret Habits are key. Until you learn to act and think like an organized person, you will continue to ride the "get-organized-and-mess-it-up-again roller coaster". And I want you off that ride! I want to teach you how to get organized so you STAY organized!

The Birth of the Secret Habits of Organized People

Back in the days when I was figuring out how to get myself organized, I had a flash of realization. Like you, I had gotten organized many times only to watch everything quickly fall back into disarray.

I knew there had to be a better way.

One day I realized I knew people who seemed so naturally organized that you could visit them unannounced and not spy a single pile of paper or be subjected to excuses for how things looked.

Being organized wasn't a big deal for these born-organized

people. They didn't have to think about being organized. It just happened naturally.

In a flash of insight I realized they knew something I didn't. And I decided to figure out exactly what it was.

I started by asking how they did it. Guess what? They couldn't tell me. They didn't know how they stayed organized. It was just second nature to them. In fact, they responded to my question with surprise. After all, it wasn't a big deal to them. They thought **everyone** knew how to stay organized.

So I started a secret study. When I visited these naturally organized people, I slyly observed how they kept their homes and offices under control. I tuned in to exactly what they did to keep the clutter from gathering.

You know what I discovered? It mostly came down to habits. They were organized and I wasn't because they just did things differently than I did.

Well, I began applying their habits to my own life. And guess what? Over time, as those habits became second nature to me, I transformed from a disorganized person to being pretty organized most of the time.

Case Study: Nora and the Roller-Coaster

Nora was a single mom who dreamed of transforming her bedroom into a calming refuge far different from the chaos and clutter pervading the rest of her house.

Instead of a refuge, her bedroom was perpetually scattered with papers and clothes and books and toys.

One quiet weekend, when her kids were with her ex-husband, Nora decided to organize her bedroom. Determined to create the peaceful sanctuary she craved, Nora cleaned out her closet, her nightstands, and her dresser drawers. She banished the wild assortment of stuff littering the floor and flat surfaces. Sunday afternoon she took a huge load of stuff to a local charity.

On Sunday evening Nora breathed a sigh of relief as she took an exhausted, yet satisfied look around her bedroom. Finally, the piles of magazines and books were off the nightstand. Her closet door could close. The chair was clear of clothes. She'd done it. Her bedroom was a peaceful, organized sanctuary.

There was one big problem, however. Nora made the same mistake most people make when they try to get organized; she neglected to change her habits.

Without changing her habits Nora would merely *get* organized. She wouldn't *stay* organized. She had started her wild ride on the organizing roller coaster.

Let's look at how Nora's habits got in the way of her desire to have a peaceful, tidy bedroom:

That same Sunday night when Nora got ready for bed she did the things she always did. She tossed her dirty clothes on the chair and left her shoes in the corner. "I'll pick them up tomorrow," she told herself. Before Nora turned out the light, she dropped the magazine she was reading onto the floor by the bed. She added that to next morning's pick up list as well. After all, the kids were still gone. She'd have time.

The next morning Nora woke up late. She didn't have time to pick up her clothes or the magazine. In her rush Nora tossed her wet towel in the corner with yesterday's shoes.

She didn't make her bed. She left her coffee cup on the dresser along with a pair of earrings. Before finally settling on what to wear, Nora draped the two outfits she tried on over the chair with yesterday's dirty clothes. Nora did all these things without noticing it. These were her habits, after all.

At the office, Nora told her buddies about her success with her bedroom. She had worked hard and was thrilled with the result. But in reality, Nora's bedroom was returning to clutter and disarray already.

Nora made a common mistake. *She got organized without changing her habits.* Until she changes her habits, all her organizing efforts will be like digging a hole in the sand.

Nora's story is typical among disorganized people. In a survey of my newsletter readers, the get-organized-only-to-mess-it-up-again experience is a common frustration.

What can we learn from Nora? Good intentions aren't enough. **To be an organized person, you must learn to act like an organized person.**

It *can* be done. *You* can do it. Don't worry. I'm right here beside you. The Secret Habits of Organized People are embedded in what you'll learn in the rest of this book. We'll talk in detail about the specific habits in Chapter 9.

Beware These Dragons

Have you ever seen one of those early maps explorers used to chart their journeys across unknown seas? Remember the dire warnings labeling the undiscovered portions of ocean: "Beware: There be dragons here!"

I've already charted the new territory of organizing into which you are about to venture. Not only do I know where the dragons are, I've battled them myself!

In my years of becoming organized and helping other people become organized, I've noticed some common patterns. These are the dragons you likely will encounter on your path to becoming

Effortlessly Organized. We certainly don't want any of these to hinder your progress, so let's talk about them now.

DRAGON #1 – BEWARE WELL-MEANING PEOPLE BEARING OLD STUFF.

Many people, even organized ones, have a hard time getting rid of their old stuff. Somehow, giving their cast-off treasures to someone they love is easier than throwing them away or donating them to a charity. They are always on the lookout for a friend or relative to take their old stuff off their hands. You, as a messy person, are a prime target for their gifts.

My own experience with this dragon came early on; when my older sister would deposit her unwanted toys in my bedroom. She would appear at my door with large boxes of junk. Of course, I adored her, and I loved getting her treasures. But, I couldn't manage my stuff, let alone hers. So her stuff merged with my stuff. The result? A colossal mess!

My dear sister, as with other folks off-loading their old stuff, meant well, she really did. But you, dear reader, have a stuff problem. Therefore, you must guard against these well-meaning types. You must not take their castoffs, no matter how tempting.

Two things are at work here,

1. The difficulty of telling someone you care about you don't want or like their castoffs, and

2. The little voice in the pit of your stomach suggesting you might be able to use the thing.

Naturally organized people have a cold and practical eye toward stuff. To free yourself from the claws of disorganization, you must develop the same cold eye. If you can't say no to your sweet Aunt Claire who insists you take her polyester pantsuit, then at the very least give it to charity immediately.

Dragon #2 – Beware of making things too complicated.

A common trait I've seen over and over with disorganized people is designing organizing systems that are too complicated.

We seem to fall in love with the idea of being organized and get swept away by our fantastic ideas – many of which are totally unrealistic or impractical. We think if we just try hard enough we'll follow through with our intentions.

It just doesn't work that way.

We put all our creative energy into setting up a system without giving a thought to how we'll maintain it. So the system collapses and once again we convince ourselves that we just can't stay organized.

Things must be simple for a disorganized person to transform into an organized person. Where a naturally organized person can follow through on the extra steps, a born disorganized person can't. Not won't, but CAN'T!

Set up your organizing systems from the start for simplicity. They must require you make the fewest decisions possible and take the fewest number of steps.

Much of what you'll learn in this book is based on this premise: for now, it's enough for you to be aware of your natural tendency to make things too complicated. Guard against it.

I recently spoke to Gene who had called in frustration about his wife. Here's what Gene told me, "My wife keeps saying 'I just have to get organized!' Then she goes on the computer and spends hours typing lists and labels that she prints out, cuts up, and pastes up around the house. She never gets to the organizing and doesn't recognize how difficult she makes even the most simple of steps."

DRAGON #3 – BEWARE OF BLINDLY ADOPTING OTHER PEOPLE'S SYSTEMS

I alluded to this under Dragon #2, so let's get to the heart of it now.

This dragon burns you when you try to do things the way an organized person would. Naturally organized people can and will take extra steps to accomplish an objective. This won't work for you.

The trick is to observe how an organized person does things and then simplify it so you can accomplish your objective.

I rarely made my bed as a kid, not because I was lazy as I was often told, but because it was too hard to do. The problem was my mom's insistence we make our beds a certain way.

We were supposed to pull the covers all the way back and air the bed for a bit before making it. That meant I was expected to return later in the morning and make the bed. NO WAY! It never happened. Not only was it impossible for me to remember to return later to make the bed, but having all the covers pulled back was entirely overwhelming.

Hence, my unmade bed was a sore spot between my mom and me for many years. Too many steps for this girl! It wasn't until I had my own apartment and developed my own easy way to make my bed, did my bed get made every day.

Do not try and do things in ways that work for other people. Your systems must work for you!

DRAGON #4 – BEWARE OF ABANDONING SYSTEMS

I see this often with my ADHD coaching clients, many of who are disorganized. Faced with changing or adjusting a system as needed, they seem to abandon it instead.

Accept your systems will change. You'll find you use a system faithfully for a while and then one day you'll stop using it. This is a sign for you to adjust the system. The problems start when you throw out the whole system instead of making tiny changes to it.

Take baby steps. Don't throw out the entire system or make huge changes when tiny adjustments would be more successful. Look at what's working, what you want the system to do for you and how you can adjust what's not working.

Dragon #5: Beware Garage Sales

On the surface, holding a garage sale may seem like a good way to get rid of clutter. You'd at least make some money from all that extra stuff you're getting rid of. A garage sale would also give you a deadline. An exact time everything has to be pushed out into the front yard ready to make you a small fortune.

So why not get organized with a garage sale?

Because a garage sale is a large project that takes planning, organization, focus, and follow through. Last time I looked, none of those were strengths of people with organization problems.

After you've dug out the stuff to sell, you've got to price things, set up, put up signs, get cash, and sit around all weekend staffing the sale. These types of little steps befuddle the disorganized mind.

However, the garage sale isn't the biggest problem! The big problem is AFTER the sale when you have to get rid of all the stuff that didn't sell.

Of course, you say you'll box up all that stuff and take it to the Goodwill. Will you really?

Here's a more likely scenario....

Exhausted from all the work of putting on the sale, you'll shove the piles of stuff that didn't sell back into the garage and vow to take it to Goodwill LATER.

When will later be? Who knows. It probably won't be soon.

Your organizing problems have suddenly multiplied like rabbits. Your garage is even more of a mess than when you started. You've added another major item to your to-do list. Another sliver of guilt is lodged in your soul. You've another thing to fight about with your spouse.

Do me a favor. If you want to clear clutter and get organized, don't impulsively have a garage sale.

POPULAR ORGANIZING MYTHS EXPOSED

Along with the Organizing Dragons we've just covered, there are a few more things you need to know about to make your organizing journey easier.

There are many naturally organized people in the world who, bless their hearts, try to be helpful by writing articles and books about how to get organized. Just one problem, many of their suggestions are helpful ONLY IF YOU ARE A NATURALLY ORGANIZED PERSON!

What's happened is some of these suggestions have been written so many times they are believed to be true for everyone – those born messy as well as those born organized. A world of myths now exists about how to be organized.

Let's expose some of these fallacies for what they are, shall we?

MYTH #1 – ONLY HANDLE PAPER ONCE

In reality it usually doesn't make sense to act on a paper the first time you handle it. It's not a good use of time or you may need to hang on to the paper, look at it, mull about it for a while before you decide what to do with it.

I mean really. Do they expect you to open the mail, pull out your checkbook, pay a bill, record it in your check book, put a stamp on the darn thing and drop it in the mail while the kids are clamoring at your feet for supper or the dog is whining to go out? (I do have one client, however, who swears it's easier to pay the bills when they arrive in the mail. Whatever works!)

Here's what you want instead:

- Quickly decide what you will do with a piece of paper even if that means putting it in a place where you'll decide later about what to do with it.

- Immediately get rid of paper you know you won't use or need. Handle the stuff you obviously don't need or want only long enough to toss it in the shredder or recycling bin.

Myth #2 – Use a tickler file to manage your 'to-dos' and paperwork

This one truly baffles me. I've even read it in some books specifically written for people with ADHD. I went so far once as taking a poll of the readers of my newsletter. I thought I was missing something. I was relieved my readers confirmed my suspicions and overwhelmingly reported that tickler files don't work for disorganized people.

In case you don't know what a tickler file is, it's a method of keeping track of the papers you need to handle each day. You use a set of files or a notebook numbered one through thirty-one for the days of the month. Papers, notes, or entire file folders are placed behind the date when you're supposed to take action on the item.

It sounds good at first glance. Except the entire system falls apart when you neglect to check the files for one or two (or more) days. Bills go unpaid, papers get lost, planned tasks are forgotten.

Tickler files are too darn easy to screw up even for reformed messies. You'll do better to create systems that can continue to function despite abuse and neglect.

MYTH #3 – TYPE YOUR FILE LABELS

I've read this myth in a couple of books. Do you suppose the labeling machine and office supply companies spread this myth?

If you have a secretary, ignore me on this one. However, for most of us, typing file labels takes too much time. It's an extra step that makes filing and changing your filing system overwhelming.

Neatly writing your labels with a good felt marker such as a Sharpie is much faster and easier.

MYTH #4 – COLOR CODE YOUR FILE SYSTEM

Here's another favorite of the filing supply companies looking to increase their sales: using different colored file folders to represent different topics will magically help you stay organized. If only it were so simple.

In reality, organizing your filing system by color adds extra steps to creating files and changing your filing system.

Suppose you use red folders for your financial papers and green for medical records. You need to add a new file for a new bank account you've opened, but you can't find a red file folder. What will you do? You'll use a green folder instead and there goes your carefully set up file system.

By all means, use colored folders if you find it makes filing more fun and your file drawers prettier. I personally adore purple and yellow files. But, stop short at assigning meaning to the colors.

MYTH #5 – USE A DAY PLANNER

You can pick the naturally organized people out of a crowd by looking for people carrying tidy day planners.

Disorganized people are truly challenged when it comes to punching holes in papers, opening binder rings and inserting the pages as day planners require.

All those extra steps mean the papers are usually shoved in the front of the day planner waiting for the first chance to fall out.

Yes, you need a calendar to plan your days and activities, but keep your system simple and make sure it suits your life style and activity level.

If your life is fairly quiet with few outside activities a basic calendar with enough room to write and a steno pad to list tasks should do it.

Myth #6 – If you had enough storage you'd be organized

Dashing out to the store to buy shelving or large plastic containers will not solve your problems. Yet that's what most people do when they think of becoming organized. They just know a new box or larger house would make the problems go away.

Actually, buying the storage boxes and shelving is one of the last things I'll have you do. In fact, if you're like most clients I've organized, in the end you'll find out you have too many storage containers.

Most people have a stuff problem and a habits problem. Not a storage problem.

If You've Gotta do Something....

Here's an opportunity for early action:

1. Get a grocery bag.
2. Start in your kitchen and fill the bag with 16 things you

can throw away. You're looking for stuff that is obvious trash. (If you fill up one bag toss it in the trash and get another bag and keep moving.)

3. When you've collected 16 things toss the bag in the garbage can.

4. Now, get back to reading this book!

CHAPTER 4 SUMMARY

KEY POINTS TO REMEMBER ABOUT LEARNING THE GROUND RULES

- Adopt **The Secret Habits of Organized People** – Replace your clutter causing habits with the habits of a naturally organized person.

- **Beware These Dragons**
    - Dragon #1 – Beware Well-Meaning People Bearing Old Stuff.
    - Dragon #2 – Beware of Making Things Too Complicated.
    - Dragon #3 – Beware of Blindly Adopting Other People's Systems.
    - Dragon #4 – Beware of Abandoning Systems.
    - Dragon #5—Beware of Garage Sales

- **Popular Organizing Myths Exposed**
    - Myth #1 – Only Handle Paper Once – FALSE!
    - Myth #2 – Use a Tickler File to Manage Your 'To-Dos' and Paperwork – FALSE!
    - Myth #3 – Type Your File Labels – FALSE!
    - Myth #4 – Color-Code Your File System – FALSE!
    - Myth #5 – Use a Day Planner – FALSE!
    - Myth #6 – If You had Enough Storage You'd be Organized – FALSE!

Review Questions

1. What keeps most people from getting Organized for Life?

   a. They don't make their bed every day.

   b. They don't have a color coded file system.

   c. They don't adopt the habits of organized people.

2. Nora's bedroom quickly fell back into disorganization because she had to go to work in the morning. ___ True   ___ False

3. If your Cousin Louise wants to give you her prized-but-ugly set of wedding china you:

   a. Run screaming from her house.

   b. Sweetly say 'No, thank you'.

   c. Take it and immediately drop it off at the Salvation Army on your way home.

   d. Take it and find space in the back of the top kitchen cabinet over the stove.

   e. B or C.

4. Making small tasks as complicated as possible is the key to being Effortlessly Organized. ___ True   ___ False

5. If you suddenly stop using a system that has worked well for you for a while you should:

   a. Abandon it totally.

   b. Call your best friend and moan about what a failure you are.

   c. Consider why you stopped using it and make tiny changes.

6. Which of these methods is best for disorganized people?

a. Only handle paper once.

b. Use a tickler file like your life depends on it.

c. Always type your file labels.

d. Color-code your file system – preferably using pastel shades.

e. Use the biggest, most complicated day planner you can find.

f. Drop whatever you're doing right now and dash to the store to buy more storage boxes.

g. All of the above.

h. None of the above.

CHAPTER 5

Step Three: Making Organizing Manageable

What question do you suppose I hear most often about getting organized? It's this: "Where do I start?"

Even after setting yourself up for success with your intention and commitment, after learning the ground rules, you're still probably facing years' worth of clutter, false starts, and discouragement.

What do you suppose is the biggest excuse I hear for why people can't get organized? "I don't have enough time!"

It's overwhelming, isn't it? Everyone and everything seems to need attention. Your job, house, kids, friends, family, husband and hopefully, you. Believe me, I understand.

That's why to be Organized for Life, all you need is 15 minutes a day. That's it. *In fact, that's all I want you to do.* Any more than 15 minutes and you'll burn out and give up.

At first, following the program will seem like one more thing. But as you make progress, you'll find you have much more time in return than an extra 15 minutes a day: time you save from not having to search for things and battle your clutter.

Are you ready to become Organized for Life? In this chapter you'll learn where to start and how taking small steps will set in motion your future of being organized for life.

From today on you will never again face the overwhelming dilemma of not knowing where to start to get organized. When you follow the steps I'm about to outline, all you'll need to know is what week of the month it is and your right hand from your left.

ROW A LITTLE EVERYDAY

I adapted this idea from a professional organizer I knew when I first started in the business many years ago. She organized offices and came up with the term ROW to help her clients remember to do a little Routing Office Work every day. I've since tweaked it a bit to mean Routine Organizing Work.

ROWing (Routine Organizing Work) is a key step to help you get organized and stay organized. When you ROW, you do a little bit of organizing every day.

Here's the deal: you are allowed to organize for just 15 minutes each day. No more. During your 15 minutes you'll take lots of small steps toward being Effortlessly Organized.

Why do I want you to ROW a little every day? The benefits are numerous:

- Your organizing job will stay mentally manageable, instead of overwhelming.

- You won't experience burnout because you'll know what you don't do today will get done tomorrow.

- You'll see gradual, more meaningful progress instead of

the 'organize and mess it up again' roller coaster.

- Everyone can find 15 extra minutes a day. You may have to watch less TV or not do the crossword puzzle, but 15 minutes a day is possible.

Right now I want you do decide WHEN each day you'll do your ROWing. First thing in the morning? At night after dinner?

Consider these things as you decide when to do your ROWing?

- What time of day is your energy best? I'm a morning person, so I do best early in the day. I grab my 15 ROWing minutes between the time my daughter leaves for school and when I get to my office at 9 AM. If I wait until later in the day or evening, the ROWing doesn't get done – *even if I have the time.*

- What habit(s) must you change to have time to ROW a little every day? I must shower and dress first thing when I get out of bed. If I stay in my bathrobe, I often neglect the ROWing. Also, if I turn on the TV to catch the morning news, I'm sunk.

- What temptations will stop you from doing your ROWing, and what will you do about them? I've found if I sit down to read the newspaper after Aja and Scott leave in the morning, I don't get to my ROWing. I read the paper over lunch or in the evening.

- How will you remember to ROW? Over time ROWing will become a habit. Until then, you'll need support. Can you get a buddy involved? Set an alarm to go off at your start time? I keep a list of my daily ROWing chores on our kitchen bulletin board to keep me on track.

If you have trouble remembering to do your ROWing, go back

to Chapter 3 and reread the Retraining Your Brain technique you learned. Use that to keep on track with your ROWing.

A Success Story

Justine had a new baby when she called. She had a 3-year-old and a 7-year-old as well. "Help! With the first two children I could manage. With the third, I'm now a stay-at-home mom. I thought since I'm no longer working, I'd have more time, but it's worse than ever. I can't seem to get anything done."

As Justine and I talked, it became clear that since she wasn't working outside the house, Justine no longer had the structure to keep organized. To create the structure she needed, Justine agreed to try two ROWing sessions a day: 15 minutes to clean after her 7-year old left for school, and 15 minutes to organize in her zone after lunch.

Within a month Justine was thrilled. "I can't believe it! In only 30-minutes a day and the house is tidy. I never knew so little time could have such an impact."

In the Zone

The Flylady, Marla Cilley, introduced me to the ideas of Zones. **Dividing your house into organizing zones is a breakthrough way to make getting organized more manageable.** I've taken Flylady's excellent system and, I think, improved upon it.

I like the Zone system for a couple of reasons. First, it helps keep your organizing project in orderly bite sized chunks. Second, each day you know where to start and focus your energy.

Just this morning I decided to do an experiment; I jumped into my ROWing purposely ignoring my Zones. The result? I bumbled around, overwhelmed and unsure of where to start. Every bit of clutter I saw caught my attention. I got frustrated and made little progress in my allotted 15 minutes.

On typical mornings when I work to my Zones, I can jump right in overlooking the parts of the house outside my Zone – it doesn't matter – I'll get to them sooner or later.

How Zones Work

In case you're unfamiliar with Flylady, here's an overview of the Zone system we'll follow. We'll nail down the details later in this chapter.

1   You divide your home into five Zones; one zone for each week of the month.

2   Each week you'll focus your organizing efforts – your ROWing - in that week's Zone.

3   Each month, starting the first of the month, you go back to Zone 1 and repeat all the zones.

4   In a few months, you will have spent time organizing in all parts and rooms of your house.

Believe me, when you spend 15 minutes a day organizing in each Zone you'll notice a difference – your house will look great.

The Zone Schedule

Here's the list of which week is spent in which Zone:

- **Zone 1** - The first day of the month through the first Sunday of the month. Depending on how the calendar falls, some months you'll spend only a day or two in Zone 1, so it needs to be a part of the house that's relatively small and easy to keep tidy.

- **Zone 2** – The first Monday of the month through the second Sunday.

- **Zone 3** – The second Monday of the month through the third Sunday.

- **Zone 4** – The third Monday of the month through the fourth Sunday.

- **Zone 5** – The fourth Monday of the month through the last day of the month.

FLYLADY'S ZONES

Flylady recommends your Zones focus on the major living areas of the house. She suggests once you've organized all the rooms in those zones you move on to focus on other areas.

Here are the Zones Flylady suggests:

- **Zone 1** – The Entry Hall, Front Porch and Dining Room

- **Zone 2** – The Kitchen

- **Zone 3** – The Bathroom and One Extra Room

- **Zone 4** – The Master Bedroom and Bathroom

- **Zone 5** – The Living Room

Though I adore Flylady's Zone idea, it has some problems:

- I find I need to include all the rooms in my house in my Zones or I never move on to the other areas. This means my Zones have more rooms, but I know everything will get looked at occasionally.

- Many contemporary homes have more rooms than the three bedrooms and two baths model – bedrooms, family rooms, dens, offices, etc. To be Organized for Life you need to design your system to match your house. Otherwise, rooms become overlooked and overlooked rooms quickly become 'junk' rooms

- Except for the front porch, Flylady concentrates primarily inside the house. Though it adds extra work, I include the outside areas readily visible from inside the house as well as areas I use or walk through frequently, such as the back porch connecting our garage and backdoor. What use is it to have the inside of the house looking nice if you're looking out the window at a messy cluttered view?

Dana's Zones

Here are the Zones I use in my house with a little explanation of why I grouped them the way I did:

- **Zone 1** – The Entry Hall, Front Porch and Dining Room. These are rather small areas, though they do collect clutter quickly if I neglect them!

- **Zone 2** – The Kitchen and Back Porch. We use our kitchen a lot, and it needs more attention than our other rooms. Since our back porch is small and right off the kitchen, I've combined these two into a Zone.

- **Zone 3** – The Bathroom, Hallway, Guest Room / Sewing Room, and our Daughter's Room. I've combined these rooms into one Zone because they are all in the same area of the house. The guest room doubles as my sewing room – it can become a junk room quick as a flash if I don't keep my eye on it!

- **Zone 4** – The Living Room, Upstairs Deck, Master Bedroom and Master Bathroom. These rooms are in the same area so I've combined them into one Zone. This is my toughest Zone. All three rooms and the deck get a lot of use from the entire family, including the dog and cat. On weeks I'm ROWing in Zone 4, I've got my hands full, and I move fast!

- **Zone 5** – The downstairs part of the house: Laundry Room, Family Room, Downstairs Deck, and my Office. All three rooms are in the basement and I'm the only one who really uses them, so they usually stay pretty tidy. One problem – the basement is a handy place to stash stuff we don't know what to do with, so occasionally it does get out of control.

Setting Up Your Zones

Okay, let's get to work setting up your Zones. Remember, these aren't cast in stone. If they aren't working for you, make adjustments.

Suggested Zones

- **Zone 1** – Remember depending on how the month falls on the calendar, you can have as little as one or two days in this Zone, so it needs to be a small one. Typically the Entry Hall, Front Porch and Dining Room are enough for Zone 1.

- **Zone 2** – The kitchen and one or two other small areas or rooms nearby. Perhaps the back porch, breakfast nook, laundry room, or powder room.

- **Zone 3** – The bedrooms and bathrooms other than the master bedroom and bath and any other adjacent rooms.

- **Zone 4** – The master bedroom and bathroom, patio, office, and any other adjacent rooms.

- **Zone 5** – The living room and family room, patio, powder room, and any other adjacent rooms.

These are merely guidelines to get you started. If it makes more sense to combine different rooms into a Zone then do so. Sometimes it makes sense, as I've done with my house, to combine the upstairs or downstairs into one Zone. Experiment and see what works for your house.

Write out your Zones and the rooms you include in each. Stick these on the refrigerator or someplace where you'll easily see it.

GROUND RULES FOR USING YOUR ZONES

- When you first start your organizing project, I want you to spend your ROWing time clearing clutter and organizing in that week's zone (you'll learn how in the next chapter).

- Set a timer and work for 15 minutes a day. That's it!! If you do more you'll burn out and give up on your goal. As your house gets organized, you can add cleaning chores to each zone.

- During your ROWing time, IGNORE clutter and messes in any Zone you're not working in that week. Use the Zones to stay focused and keep your project manageable.

- Unless your religion prohibits you from working on Saturday or Sunday, I suggest you spend 15 minutes in your Zone every day of the week. I've found taking Sunday or the weekend off breaks the habit and makes it hard to pick it up again.

- Find a convenient time of day that works for you and your schedule to do your ROWing.

ROW RIGHT

One of the questions I'm asked most frequently is "where do I start"?

This is easy. All you have to remember is to ROW Right. ROWing Right is so simple, I'm almost embarrassed to tell you, but it works on all kinds of organizing projects – big and small.

To ROW Right you simply go to the area you want to organize – a Zone or a room – walk in the door and turn right. Start clearing clutter and organizing stuff and keep moving around the room to the right (the room's right – not yours). When your 15 minutes for the day is done you stop. The next day or time you work on that room or Zone, just start where you left off and keep moving to the right.

Why does ROWing Right work? It keeps you from falling into two organizing traps.

- Not starting because you don't know where to start, and

- Bouncing all over the house so you don't seem to make much progress and nothing ever gets done.

Rowing Right is a fine technique for almost any organizing project; clearing a closet, cleaning off the kitchen counter after dinner, clearing your desk at work, or cleaning out a drawer. Simply start at one end and move to the right.

Use a Timer

A timer is an important tool for getting and staying organized. It's what keeps you on track for your daily 15-minute ROWing time.

Although there are different types of timers you can use, I recommend a timer that you can carry with you easily. For instance, I use a wristwatch timer. Since I started wearing it, I've discovered lots of creative ways to put it to work. And my life runs much more smoothly as a result.

Here are a few other ideas on how you can put timers to work in your daily routines:

- Break big, daunting, icky jobs down into small chunks of time. For example, if I think I need to spend an hour organizing files, I won't do it. But if I set my timer for 15 minutes and commit to doing only what I can do in that time, I can handle it. Remember, even 15 minutes makes progress toward getting something done.

- Depart on time. When I need to leave for an appointment in 25 minutes, I simply set my timer for 20 minutes and I'm out the door right on schedule.

- Enjoy your siesta. My after-lunch nap is a lovely part of my day but I can't let it eat up my whole afternoon. I set my timer for 15 minutes and get enough of a snooze to keep me perky until bedtime.

- Get your child out of the bathtub. As a mom I use my timer for tracking and managing all kinds of everyday events, from bath time play to timeouts. As a bonus, it helps my daughter learn about time, tasks and limits in a meaningful, consistent way.

Reliable, inexpensive timers are easy to find. Check any sporting goods store or large retailer. Or you can even shop from the convenience of your home on the internet.

The Two-Minute Rule

You're about to learn a very powerful technique for staying organized; even if you have adult ADHD. Use this trick consistently and, overtime, much of the clutter in your home and office will disappear.

The secret is getting organized in a way that suits ADHD's impulsive and spontaneous nature. That's why I like little tricks that make organizing practically natural.

Here's one of my all-time favorite organizing tricks.

I call it the Two-Minute Rule. Surefire organizing tricks to help even the most unfocused of us conquer disorganization and get things done.

The Two-Minute Rule is incredibly simple: when you notice a task you can do in two minutes or less, do it when you think of it.

That's all there is to it.

How to Conquer Procrastination With The Two-Minute Rule

1. You notice something that needs to be done.

2. Quickly decide if it can be done in less than two minutes.

3. If you can do it in two minutes or less then you do it!

The Two-Minute Rule makes life easier both at work and at home. Papers get filed, phone calls get made, dishes get rinsed and put in the dishwasher, junk mail gets recycled, and clothes get hung up instead of tossed on the floor.

Here's An Example

You remember you need to make a dentist appointment. The typical ADHD approach? Do it later.

The Two-Minute Rule approach? Look up the number, pick up the phone and schedule the appointment. When you've made the appointment, instead of waiting to add it to your calendar, you do it on the spot. After all, it will take less than two minutes to do.

What if you really don't have two minutes right then or you know something will take longer than that to do? Write it on your To Do List.

However, adding a task to your To Do List is the last resort. Why put something on your To Do List when doing it takes just a smidgen more time? Follow the Two-Minute Rule and take care of things when you notice them.

As I've tested out the Two-Minute Rule over the past few months, I've been reminded how organizing is like a muscle. The more you use small organizing tricks the stronger your organizing muscle gets.

If You've Still Gotta do Something....

Here's another opportunity for early action:

1   Get a grocery bag

2   Starting in the messiest room of the house, fill the bag with 16 things you can throw away. You're looking for stuff that is obvious trash (if you fill up one bag toss it in the trash and get another bag). When you get to 16 things, throw it all away.

3   Now, get back to reading this book!

CHAPTER 5 SUMMARY

KEY POINTS TO REMEMBER ABOUT MAKING ORGANIZING MANAGEABLE

- **ROW a Little Everyday** – spend 15 minutes daily doing your Routine Organizing Work.

- **Divide your house into five organizing zones** and concentrate on one zone at a time to make staying organized more manageable.

- **ROW Right** to make organizing easy to know where to start. Simply go into the area you want to organize, turn right, and start organizing around the room moving to the right.

- **Use a Timer** to stay on track during your 15-minutes of ROWing.

REVIEW QUESTIONS

1 ROWing a little every day means doing 15-minutes of Routine Organizing Work each day. ____ True   ____ False

2 What time each day will you do your ROWing? Write it here:

3 How will you remember to do your ROWing every day?

4 What could stop you from ROWing and what will you do about it?

5 List which rooms you'll include in each of your **Zones**:

   – Zone 1:

   – Zone 2:

- – Zone 3:

- – Zone 4:

- – Zone 5:

6   What organizing trap does **ROWing Right** keep you from falling into?

7   How will you use your **timer**? If you don't yet have a timer, get one next time you're out.

CHAPTER 6

Step Four: Digging out – Get Control of the Clutter

C lutter is a major roadblock if you want to be organized. Clutter takes over your home and your life. Extra stuff costs money to store and takes time to tend. Clutter is confusing, overwhelming, and depressing.

To be organized for life you must zap clutter. Simple. No excuses. You can't have an Effortlessly Organized life if you're surrounded by piles of unneeded stuff.

What actually is clutter, anyway? Clutter is:

- Anything you own that you don't use or love
- Anything you own that doesn't have a "home" (a place to be put away)
- Anything you own that isn't put away

The number one rule about clutter is this – if you don't like something, or use it, or need it to stay out of prison, get rid of it.

I don't care how much money you spent on it or who gave it to you. If you don't like or use something, it is sucking your time and energy away from more fun and rewarding activities. Of course, keep stuff like tax records that could cause you legal trouble if need them.

Please don't think I take the challenge of clutter lightly. I've seen clutter's effect in my life and in the life of people I work with. I've been ridiculed and ashamed because of my own mess.

As a professional organizer, I saw the worst. Houses piled high with all manner of things. Offices so full of old magazines and files a small path was the only means to move around the room.

Once, I encountered a black widow spider living in a stack of files next to a client's desk! (Frankly, I still believe I deserve an Academy Award for the calm, casual way I killed the spider and acted as though I frequently found black widows in people's offices.)

I've heard wise and wonderfully talented people belittled by their spouses because they didn't know how to get rid their stuff.

I've seen the shame in the eyes of smart, generous, delightful people who live in terror that someone will discover how they live. Many people with ADHD live with clutter because they can't make decisions or get so distracted they rarely finish anything or put things away.

The reasons people keep clutter can be very complex. The junk itself is only the physical aspect of the problem.

Sometimes clutter is the sign of severe psychological problems – ruinous shopping addictions or chronic hording. The techniques and tips for clearing clutter in this chapter are intended for people who can get rid of things with the right suggestions and support, even though they're challenged by their accumulation of stuff.

The wood of your dining room table may be hidden from view or your office may be covered in papers and files, but it's because you get overwhelmed or don't know where to start; not because you can't get rid of anything.

If you are someone who has a panic attack at the thought of throwing anything out then please seek appropriate medical help.

When it comes to clutter, naturally organized people show no mercy. They know clutter wastes time and energy. They know clutter makes cleaning harder and life more stressful. So if you're aiming to live like an organized person, you must learn to clear clutter with a vengeance.

Unfortunately, clearing clutter presents a major roadblock for many disorganized people. How do you know what to get rid of? What do you do with it? Why does clutter reappear so quickly even when banished?

To get control of your clutter, you'll need to know:

- How to clear clutter
- How to keep clutter from accumulating

What? I'm not mentioning storage here? Nope. That's after you clear the clutter. As Marla Cilley, the FlyLady, is fond of saying in her book *"Sink Reflections"*, you can't organize clutter!

Let's get started, shall we?

How to Clear Clutter

Divide and Conquer – One Piece at a Time

I'll admit it, ridding your world of clutter can be tedious and overwhelming.

However, much of the problem is how you view your clutter. Don't worry; I'm not going to ask you to become one with your clutter. I just want you to look at it a different way. We give clutter too much power. It's really only pieces of stuff that you need to get rid of or put away.

What's the biggest problem with clutter? We tend to look at it as one huge mass. But it truly isn't.

Granted, the project of getting rid of the clutter may be large. But clutter is actually composed of lots of little pieces of stuff.

That pile right there by your side – yes, THAT pile – is really just a stack of lots of little things.

And when you get down to it, there aren't that many things to do with each thing in that pile. You can:

1. Throw it away,

2. Give it away,

3. Put it away, or

4. Decide where to keep it.

Four choices. That's it. **I know you can do this.**

You must stop looking at your piles as though you have to get rid of it all right now. Little steps. The clutter didn't accumulate in one day and you won't get rid of it in one day, either.

People digging out from the grip of clutter often expect too much. Even though you know it is unrealistic, deep down you probably think you have to get rid of all the clutter right now.

Poof! – the dining room table must be clear. Poof! – the clothes must all be off the bedroom floor.

Clearing clutter is like a muscle; you need to strengthen the muscle before it can do its best work for you.

Trust me on this. I've seen it over and over in my life and in the lives of my organizing clients.

Over time, you will find you can get rid of many things you want to hang on to now. The more you practice clearing clutter, the easier you'll find it to look at something and say, "You're outta here!"

It took me three years to rid my home of clutter. I got rid of the easy stuff first and gradually cleared out the rest of the things I didn't like or use.

Yes, sometimes clutter builds up again. When it does, I refocus on clearing it out.

I recently got a call from Dave, a former organizing client. For years we'd struggled to rid Dave's office of unneeded magazines, old newspapers and out of date files.

One day, out of the blue, Dave called to report that *finally* he had reached the point where he no longer felt compelled to hang on to unnecessary, old papers and articles. The stacks of stuff were gone from his floor, cabinets, and desk. He no longer dreaded going into his office and no longer lived in fear that the quality of his work would be judged by the cleanliness of his desk.

I want you to understand that clearing clutter is a step-by-step process and the more you do it, the easier it will become.

First, you will start clearing the visible surfaces of the obvious junk. Over time you will dig deeper into drawers and cupboards – all the time ridding your world of things you don't like and don't use.

Key Questions for Clearing Clutter

Here are the questions to help you decide what to get rid of and what to keep. Print these out, write them out. Do what you must to follow them.

- Do I like this?

- How will I use this?

- Could a charity use it more than I?

- What's the worst that could happen if I got rid of it and I need it later?

Everything you do not like or use MUST be thrown away or given away.

You may have the urge to give a garage sale or to try and sell the stuff on eBay. Do this ONLY if you have an organized person in your world to help you plan and carry out your plan.

For most disorganized people, holding garage sales is merely a distraction on the road to getting organized. Plus, you have the challenge of what to do with the leftover stuff no one bought. When you hold a garage sale, you run a huge risk of your stuff coming back into your house again. Is it worth that risk? For more information on why a garage sale isn't always the greatest idea, refer to *Beware these Dragons: Dragon #5—Garage Sales*.

WHAT TO DO WITH SENTIMENTAL STUFF

Many messy people are sentimental. I certainly am. We attach deep memories to stuff. Old photos. Letters. Vacation souvenirs. The baby clothes their now-grown children wore. Everything has meaning.

I don't want you to get rid of the truly important sentimental stuff. Get rid of the obvious junk so you have room to keep the sentimental things.

I suggest you use memory boxes for the sentimental things. Buy a pretty box or gift-wrap a paper box (a memory box MUST have a lid). Put only the best, most important things in it.

HOW TO KEEP CLUTTER FROM ACCUMULATING

All right. Clearing clutter is just half the solution for living clutter free. The other part is keeping clutter from accumulating in the first place. Let's talk about how to keep the onslaught of clutter at bay.

BEWARE CLUTTER MAGNETS

Clutter magnets are those charming areas destined to magically attract a mess. Bedroom chairs, entry hall tables, kitchen counters, file cabinet tops, dining room tables, desk corners: typical clutter magnets all.

To banish clutter you must view clutter magnets as favorably as you do a plague.

You've got four options for dealing with clutter magnets.

Eliminate All Clutter Magnets You Can. Remove that chair from your bedroom. I mean it. Can you honestly remember the last time you sat in it? Or even saw it? Most bedroom chairs are piled with clothes for the dry cleaner, magazines, books, and, well…you get the idea.

Block Off Clutter Magnets. Make it harder to put stuff on the Clutter Magnet than to put stuff away. Get creative. Put photos or plants on top of the filing cabinet or the entry hall table.

Figure Out Why Clutter Gathers There. What you're doing here is addressing the root of the problem of why this Clutter Magnet attracts here.

Study what gathers on the Clutter Magnet. Where does it come from? Why? Can you spot a pattern? Is it a matter of not enough storage in the right place or bad habits? What can you do to create a solution?

Clutter often gathers when the stuff doesn't have an easy-to-use place where it belongs – a home. You'll learn all about creating excellent homes for your stuff in Chapter 7.

Create Routines for Clearing Off Clutter Magnets. If none of the above options work, dedicate a couple of minutes a day or a few minutes a week to clearing your Clutter Magnets.

You'll still have the problem, but hopefully this will keep too much stuff from accumulating. Visualizing Neat is helpful here. Keep the picture in your mind of how you want a Clutter Magnet to look to encourage you to keep it clear.

The Case of the Cluttered Counter

When our daughter started preschool, the kitchen counter by our back door suddenly transformed into a clutter magnet.

When I took a close look at the stuff accumulating on the counter, I discovered it was mostly artwork and craft projects. Everyday she'd bring more 'treasures' home from school.

Here's how the art treasures ended up on the counter:

After picking our daughter up from preschool, my husband or I would come in from the garage with our hands full of jackets, artwork, stuffed animals, groceries, briefcases, purses, etc. We'd set everything on the counter and then put away the things that had homes. Usually the only stuff left on the counter was our daughter's artwork and craft projects.

The artwork and craft projects posed two problems. First, they didn't have a home. Second, they required a decision we weren't ready to make. Some of the artwork were treasures we'd want to keep or send to grandma. Some we knew we could toss, yet we never knew when our daughter would go looking for it in a day or two and we didn't want her finding her creations in the recycling bin.

Here's how I transformed the spot from a clutter magnet back into a kitchen counter.

After considering the options, I cleared out a seldom-used kitchen drawer and turned it into an art storage bin. Now we just sweep the artwork off the counter into the drawer. Aja, our daughter, can go through it and find what she's looking for, and it no longer clutters our counter space.

When the drawer is too full to hold anything else, I quickly clear out the obvious junk and move the few treasures to a more permanent artwork home on the top shelf of her closet.

STOP CLUTTER AT THE SOURCE

This sounds like such common sense, I feel silly including it. However, often common sense isn't very common. So here we are.

Where does clutter come from? The answer is different for everyone; however, I've noticed some common patterns.

"I Might Need It Sometime"

One statement I often hear is, "the minute I get rid of something, I need it again". Well, that's a risk you'll have to take if you really want a clutter-free life.

Unless it is something so rare that you won't ever be able to replace it, I challenge you to walk on the wild side. Take a chance and get rid of things with the idea that if you do need it again you can replace it.

A favorite example comes from one of my organizing workshops. One woman confessed her aunt had a box on her shelf labeled 'String Too Short to Use'! If the string was too short to use, why do you suppose she was keeping it?

Stop what you're doing right now. It's time to take the **Won't**

Keep it Pledge. Raise your right hand and repeat after me:

"I promise never to keep something just because I might need it sometime."

There. I feel better already. Do you?

"It's Inherited"

Often, when people we love die, we end up inheriting some of their possessions.

Some of my favorite treasures once belonged to my grandmother, my great uncle, and other relatives; fond reminders of the people I now miss deeply. If you're not careful, however, inherited treasures can become clutter problems.

As an organizer, I was occasionally called upon to help organize homes overrun by inherited stuff. One situation I remember vividly was the large, lovely home of a woman named Leslie whose mother had died a few months earlier.

Leslie's grown children were coming to visit and she was in a panic. After her mother's death, Leslie and her brother had cleaned out their mother's condominium and donated a lot to charity. Not knowing what to do with their mother's prized possessions, they stashed them in Leslie's guest rooms to deal with later.

Later had finally arrived and Leslie found her guestrooms so jammed with her mother's stuff her children would have no place to sleep.

We sorted through furniture, books, photos, papers, silver, and all manner of household items. We creatively merged what we could into Leslie's home, set aside a few nice things for her children to take, boxed the most meaningful papers and photos in a large attractive basket that looked great in the guest room, and gave the rest to charity.

Leslie found the work wrenching, but with gentle guidance she was able to realize that getting rid of her mother's stuff wasn't a sign of disrespect.

Here's my recommendation for handling inherited stuff:

- **Allow only the things you love and will use into your house.** I moved my great-uncle's favorite chair and reading light into our family room. It looks fine there and I can snuggle in and feel embraced in his gentle strength and keen sense of humor. We enjoy using my husband's grandmother's china as special dessert plates.

- **Consider creative ways to use your loved one's household items.** My grandmother's eggcup has become my office paperclip holder; her coffee mug, my water cup. On dressy occasions I use Grandma's delicately embroidered evening bag and her shawl.

- Papers and photos can present a problem. **As with your own sentimental stuff save only the things that mean the most to you.** Photos of people or trips you remember, meaningful letters and certificates. Box them up so you can look through them when you wish.

- **Get help from a kind friend or a professional organizer if you find yourself stuck.** These difficult decisions are sometimes best faced with a supportive companion.

- **Avoid leaving valuables sitting in a back room gathering dust.** Find a way to sell the valuable stuff or donate it to a charity to handle for you.

"I Bought It so I Must Keep It"

Do you know anyone who says this? "I paid good money for

this [*insert item here*] so I'm going to keep it." Gosh, I sure do. So there they sit surrounded by their stuff, and dragged down by it, too.

Dare I risk sounding like a broken record? If you don't like something or don't use it, I don't care how much money it is worth or how much you paid for it! Holding on to it is costing you emotionally. Get rid of it.

"It Was Given to Me or Sent to Me so I Must Use It or Keep It"

This one goes hand in hand with *I bought it so I must keep it* above. Suppose you keep the ugly sweater your mother gave you? If you wear it you will feel ugly and each time you look at it you will feel guilty. Someone somewhere will love it. Donate it to a charity. If you must, keep it long enough for your mother to see you wearing it and then give it away.

"It Arrived in the Mail"

I once had a client who couldn't get rid of magazines or newspapers. He was afraid he would miss something by not reading it all. Hence, his office was piled high in dusty old, UNREAD magazines and copies of the Wall Street Journal.

Over time he realized he could get any of the information off the Internet if he needed it. Eventually, he cancelled all but his two favorite subscriptions. Wow, did that make his life easier!

I know people who feel they must carefully read all the junk mail they receive. Just because someone sent it to you doesn't mean you have to read it.

Better yet, get your name taken off mailing lists. I've done this and it really works! Register with the Direct Marketing Association to stop junk mail from coming to your home. Also, ask any banks, credit card companies and businesses you do business with not to sell your name in their mailing lists.

"Know Your Clutter Weaknesses"

I've noticed most people with a clutter problem have what I call *Clutter Weaknesses.*

A Clutter Weakness is something you can't resist buying or bringing into your home. You see it and you want it. Without thinking you get it.

Messy people often have more than one Clutter Weakness. Some Clutter Weaknesses I've witnessed are: extension cords, brief cases, anything from a garage sale, clothes, dishes, lipstick, books, and toys among many other possibilities.

For one client, Karen, garage sales and thrift stores were her Clutter Weakness. As an art teacher, she was always on the lookout for interesting goodies and gadgets to use in class projects.

However, Karen had a basement and studio full of craft supplies she hadn't used. She made a commitment to stay away from her Clutter Weaknesses and use only what she had on hand.

At first Karen struggled to keep her commitment, but ultimately she overcame her urge to stock up at garage sales. Besides cutting the clutter, Karen saved loads of time and money on stuff she didn't need.

My big Clutter Weakness is plants. I adore gardening and can get carried away selecting flowers and plants at nurseries and plant sales. I have learned the hard way I must have a strong, realistic discussion with myself before heading to the cashier, otherwise I come home with plants I don't have room for or time to plant. I can't begin to tell you the number of times I've said, "Dana, you don't need that" and returned plants to the shelf on which I found them.

Another Clutter Weakness I've gotten over is craft projects. When I was younger I would optimistically start a needlework project and never finish it. Finally, one day I got my mom and sister to finish some and gave away most of the rest of the projects – half done!

To stop clutter at its source you must tell the truth about your Clutter Weaknesses. Denial stops today.

"If I Ignore It, It will go Away"

A big cause of clutter is not having savvy ways to regularly handle and clear out the stuff that comes into your house. Just hoping and ignoring the clutter does not make it go away.

Stuff WILL come into your home; it's a fact of life. It comes in the mail. It comes home with you and your kids. It comes as gifts.

Ignoring clutter only allows it to pile up. You MUST regularly go through and get rid of the stuff you no longer want or need. I wish I could give you a magic wand for this, but I can't.

One trick that's really helped my family is to have our house on the pick-up route for one of our local charity thrift shops. Every couple of months I get a call from a nice lady announcing the charity will have a truck in our neighborhood on such and such a date if we have anything we'd like to donate. We always say, "Yes!" That way we have a deadline for cruising through our stuff and pulling out things to give away. We always seem to find two or three bags worth of things to send on to someone who needs them more than we do.

"Unrealistic Expectations for What You Can / Will or Need to Do"

Remember the craft Clutter Weakness I mentioned above? Well, in my case, craft projects fall under this source of clutter, too.

You see I have great expectations for what craft projects I'll complete. Over time I've learned if a project is too big – such as a large needlepoint – I won't finish it.

I also get very stuck if I don't know how to do part of a project. I've let sewing projects languish in a drawer for years for lack of clarity on the next step.

Do you have unrealistic expectations for what you can and will do? Do you think you SHOULD put all those photos in scrapbooks but you don't so they sit in piles on the shelf?

Do you think you SHOULD read all those cook books but you never do so they gather dust on the kitchen counter?

Remember my #1 rule – **NO SHOULDING ON YOURSELF!**

When it comes to clutter (and the rest of life) honesty is the best policy.

- What do you really have the time to do?
- What are you truly inclined to do?
- What do you like to do?
- What do you have space to keep?

Unrealistic expectations merely set you up for later struggles with too much stuff.

USE THESE IMPORTANT CLUTTER BASHING TOOLS

- **A large trash can with a flip lid or no lid.** As my

organizer friend, Coach Linda Anderson, calls it, "a large hungry trash can".

I once organized the house of a family who had trash overflowing all over the family room floor. Why? A family of five had a tiny trash can in one of the busiest rooms of the house right by the table where their kids did their homework. I suggested a larger can and POOF! The problem was solved (they thought I was a genius).

- **A shredder close at hand**. Shred papers as you go.

- Always have **an active 'give away' box or bag** to fill as you go. We keep ours in the coat closet.

LIMIT HOW MUCH YOU CAN KEEP

I believe there is some rule of physics along the line of *stuff expands according to how much room you allot for it*. Therefore, to win the war against clutter you MUST not give clutter too much space in which to expand.

This is especially true for things stored horizontally (flat). Why? Because, horizontal (flat) piles of paper, clothes, magazines, books - you name it - will grow and grow until they reach the ceiling. A scary thought.

However, by taking that same pile and storing it vertically (on its side) in some sort of a container, you outsmart that sneaky law of nature. You set an automatic limit for how much you can keep. Plus, with upright storage, when the storage container is full that's your cue that it's time to sort and purge the extra stuff.

Here are some ideas for limiting how much you can keep:

- Using baskets, boxes, and other containers to store things vertically (upright) limits the space available for stuff to expand and helps control the mess.

- Keeping the catalogs upright in a basket limits the number you can keep. Keeping books on a bookshelf does the same. Papers in file-folders as well.

- Keeping pencils and pens in a cup or jar makes it easier to find what you need and stops them from rolling around in your desk drawer.

Look around. Where can you store things on their sides instead of flat in a pile?

With things stored on their sides, you'll know it's time to do some clearing when:

- You can't get your hand in the file cabinet. Clean out the folders.

- You can't get another catalog in the catalog basket. Toss some of the old ones.

- You can't get another bottle of nail polish in the box. Get rid of the polish you no longer use or like.

My Favorite Trick for Quickly Zapping Clutter

I got this easy and fun clutter-blasting trick, the *27-Thing Fling*, from FlyLady. I've modified it a bit to be even more powerful.

When you 27-Thing Fling, you race around your house looking for 27 things to throw away. I've expanded it to include 27 things to give away and 27 things to put away. The power is in making it a race and focusing on finding 27 things instead of worrying about what the things are.

Here's how to 27-Thing Fling:

1   Get a bag - a plastic grocery sack will do.

2   Dash around your house or your week's zone and fill the bag with **27 things you can throw away.** Keep your eye open for things like scraps of paper and broken crayons and toys. They all count.

3   When you have 27 things in the bag, take it right outside and toss it in the trash.

4   Now get another bag and dash around filling the bag with **27 things you no longer like or use that someone else might.**

5   When the bag has 27 things in it take it right to your car and drop it by your favorite charity next time you're out.

6   Now get another bag and dash around filling the bag with **27 things you can put away.**

7   When you've collected your 27 things, take the bag around your house and empty it. Putting away the things you've collected where they belong.

A few 27-Thing Flings a week and before you know it you'll be on the road to living clutter free!

Ready, Set, Start Clearing Clutter!

Finally, it's time to dig in and attack your clutter. Only proceed to this important step of clearing clutter AFTER you've done the work in *Chapter 5 – Making Organizing More Manageable.*

Step One: *The first few times you ROW in a zone, all I want you to do are 27-Thing Flings* to get rid of the things you can easily put away, throw away and give away. When you've cleared out the 'easy pickings' proceed to Step Two.

Step Two: *Now it's time to ROW Right.* Enter the Zone for that week, turn to the right and start clearing clutter one small section at a time. Spend your ROWing time (15 minutes) and stop for the day. Set your timer.

The next day start where you left off the day before and keep working in small sections to the right. Eventually you'll have all the clutter cleared around the zone and you start at the beginning again and follow the same path.

On each pass through the zone you'll find you clear more clutter, more quickly. Things you couldn't bear to part with last time, you may be ready to give up now.

Here's Your ROW Right Game Plan:

- Get three grocery sacks. Label one *throw away*, label one *put away*, and label one *give away*.

- Select a pile to clear and set your timer for 15 minutes.

    Pick up the first thing on top of the pile and ask your clutter clearing questions:

    1. Do I like this?

    2. How will I use this?

    3. Could a charity use it more than I?

    4. What would happen if I needed it and didn't have it?

- Put everything you do not like or use in either the throw away sack or in the give away sack (if a charity could sell it or use it). If it is something you do like or will use put it in the put away sack.

- When the timer goes off after 15 minutes here's what you do:

    o Put the throw away sack in the garbage can outside. IMPORTANT WARNING: DUMPSTER DIVING IS FORBIDDEN FOR YOU AND YOUR FAMILY. (In fact don't even tell your family you are doing this or they will go into the garbage and pull things out.)

o   Put the give away sack in your car to drop off at the nearest thrift store next time you are out.

o   Look through the put away sack. Everything you can put away easily, do so. Leave things you don't know where to put in the sack – we'll deal with those later on.

RECOMMENDED RESOURCE

My favorite book about clutter (other than this one, of course) is *Clear Your Clutter with Feng Shui* by Karen Kingston.

Whether you're into Feng Shui (the Asian art of placement) or not, this book is an extremely useful and unique look at clutter and its impact on your world. This book helped me look at my stuff in a different light and let go of many things I really didn't need or like.

Kingston presents her ideas clearly with many thoughtful suggestions. She talks about the emotional reasons we keep things and what to do about them. She covers every type of clutter, from old stereo equipment, books and CD collections, kitchen appliances and cookware, to clothing and broken stuff you'll never fix.

Where Do I Start?

Let's face it. You're probably looking at that desk, dresser, or bathroom counter and thinking, "How am I going to do this?"

Don't get overwhelmed yet, though. Here is a brilliantly simple trick to remind you that you're only rowing a tiny bit every day, not tackling the whole thing at once!

This organizing trick works great when you're faced with a major area of clutter such as your desk, a table, bed, floor or counter. Any place where you're so totally overwhelmed by the piles of paper, clothes or other stuff you just don't know where to start.

All you need is an old sheet, blanket, or towel.

Here's how it works…

1. Drape a sheet or blanket over MOST of the area you are organizing. All you want showing is a small chunk of the clutter.

2. Next, clear that bit of visible clutter.

3. Once you've organized the first bit, slide the sheet over to expose another chunk of clutter, tackling it as you did in Step 2 above.

4. Keep moving the sheet, clearing and organizing as you go.

Now, isn't that simple! Just the way we like getting organized to be.

Especially if you find wrestling disorganization a daily battle like it is with so many people with Attention Deficit.

You just gotta love little tricks like this. I know I do.

Why is This Such a Stellar ADHD Organizing Tip?

Well, it makes getting organized a game, which makes it easier for stimulation-seeking brains like ours to swallow.

Also, a huge part of the challenge with disorganization is overwhelm. By limiting what you can see and tackling the mess a bit at a time, you'll be more likely to bust through the overwhelm and make progress.

CHAPTER 6 SUMMARY

KEY POINTS TO REMEMBER ABOUT DIGGING OUT AND GETTING CONTROL OF THE CLUTTER

- To be Organized for Life **you MUST ZAP clutter.**

- **Clutter** is:
  - Anything you own that you don't use or love.
  - Anything you own that doesn't have a place to be put away.
  - Anything you own that isn't put away.

- **Clutter's #1 Rule:** If you don't like it, use it, or need it to stay out of prison, GET RID OF IT!

- How **To Clear Clutter:**
  - **Divide and Conquer** – tackle clutter one piece at a time

- **Key Questions for Clearing Clutter**
  - Do I like this?
  - How will I use this?
  - Could a charity make better use of it than I?
  - What's the worst thing that could happen if I got rid of it and I needed it someday?

- To Keep Clutter from Accumulating, YOU MUST **Beware of Clutter Magnets** (areas that magically attract a clutter)!

- Four Options for **Dealing with Clutter Magnets**

1. Eliminate every clutter magnet you can.

2. Block off clutter magnets.

3. Figure out why clutter gathers there and address the root of the problem.

4. Create routines for clearing off clutter magnets.

- **The Sources of Clutter:**

  - You think you might need it sometime.

  - You inherited it.

  - You bought it so you think you must keep it.

  - It was given to you or sent to you so you think you must keep it.

  - It arrived in the mail (so you think you must keep it).

  - You don't have control of your Clutter Weaknesses.

  - You simply just don't know what to do about it.

  - You've unrealistic expectations for what you can do, will do, or need to do.

  - Important **Clutter Bashing Tools**

  - A large trash can with a flip lid or no lid.

  - A shredder.

  - An active give away bag or box.

  - Set limits for how much you can keep.

  - Quickly zap clutter with the 27-Thing Fling.

Review Questions

1. Clutter is:

   a   Anything you own that you don't use or love.

b   Anything you own that doesn't have a home.

c   Anything you own that isn't put away.

d   All of the above.

2. What's the #1 rule about clutter?

3. What Four things can you do with clutter?

4. You can expect to rid your home of all the clutter in one afternoon _____True   _____False

5. List the seven most obvious **Clutter Magnets** in your home. What will you do to deal with them?

    1.

    2.

    3.

    4.

    5.

    6.

    7.

6. What are your **Clutter Weaknesses**? What can (and will) you do to control them?

7. Right now! Get up and do a **27-Thing Fling**!

Part Three

Deciding Where to Keep Things

Chapter 7

Step Five: Everything Needs a Good Home

Like many messy people, I grew up thinking I was lazy. My laziness explained why my bedroom was a disaster area of strewn clothes, toys, and books.

One day, when I was an adult, I made a huge discovery. If something was easy to do there was a good chance I would do it. Wow! I wasn't lazy after all! The problem wasn't with me. The problem was with the system. This was the beginning of Effortless Organizing.

Have you ever thought about WHY you don't put things away? I'm not talking about some supposed character flaw you've likely been told you have such as "You're lazy," or "You're such a slob." I'm talking about the REAL reason you struggle to do something. These are problems like "The task is too hard," or "I'm not sure where this goes." So your things easily get tossed to the side or ignored.

Now it's time to figure out where to keep the things you've decided to keep; the items that deserve a place in your home because you love them or use them. We've ignored this step until now because this is easier to do after the bulk of the clutter is gone.

Deciding the best place to keep things is an important, yet often overlooked, step in getting organized. It's one of the keystones of Effortless Organizing.

If you find it too hard to decide where to keep something or too difficult to put away you won't do it. Our intent here is to find the best, easiest, most useful homes for your stuff.

Please pay attention. This is important. **To be Organized for Life you must embrace and live by this rule: Give everything a good home.**

That's right. Everything you own needs a good home.

If your things are homeless, you will live in clutter. Think about it. If you don't know where something belongs how can you realistically expect to put it away? If your things don't have good homes, you'll be more likely to leave them sitting out and clutter will reign.

Why is giving everything a good home so important? Because when your stuff has good homes:

- It's easier to put things away, so you're more apt to do so.
- You can find things more easily when you need them.

And that, ladies and gentlemen, is the key to being so Effortlessly Organized that you Stay Organized for Life!

A Good Home Defined

- **A home** is a designated place where something belongs.

No matter how disorganized you might be, you already have homes for loads of your stuff. The silverware lives in the silverware drawer, your toothbrush lives by your bathroom sink, the laundry detergent lives by the washer. Get the picture?

- **A good home** is one that's easy to remember and suits how often you use something.

- A good home makes sense and feels right. By the time you finish reading this chapter you'll know everything you need to know about creating good homes for your stuff.

- **Easy storage** involves deciding what your stuff will live in. In some respects, homes and storage are closely related. But in others, they are different. Creating easy storage is the second part. Your first step is deciding where your stuff will live; your second step is deciding how you will store it.

CASE STUDY: GOOD HOMES IN ACTION

To help you understand the difference a good home can make, here's an example from my life: One evening my husband was cooking dinner and needed some fresh rosemary for a lovely stew he was concocting. Now, he may be Head Chef in our house, but I'm Head Gardener, so it was my job to collect the rosemary from the garden even though it was a cold, winter night.

First, I needed my gardening clippers and they were exactly where they belonged in their good home at the front of my gardening tool shelf. Sure, the clippers are in a rather messy bucket with my gloves and trowels but that works for me. I can always find them and can put them away in a flash.

Second, the rosemary bush has a home (obvious, but I'm making a point here). It was dark and snowing but I knew exactly where the rosemary plants live, so it took about a minute to grab my clippers, cut the rosemary, return the clippers to their home and deliver the rosemary to my favorite chef.

I can't stress this enough. ***Having good homes for your things means you can find things easily and put them away.*** So, even if the clutter piles up a bit, you can clear it up in a jiffy without a huge struggle.

DON'T MAKE THIS COMMON MISTAKE!

Do not dash out and buy all kinds of organizing gadgets and gizmos. As tempting as it may be, that's the last thing I want you to do.

Why? Because the organizing supplies you purchase today often become the clutter you dispose of tomorrow.

Before you buy anything, I want you to make sure you need it. Patience. You still need to do and know a bit more before thinking about storage.

TYPES OF HOMES

Homes come in all shapes and sizes. Be creative when assigning homes. Use your imagination. Consider boxes, bins, baskets, shelves, drawers, file cabinets, binders, hooks, and cupboards. A home could be a corner for leaning something or a space for an item to sit on the counter.

And don't overlook the garbage can, recycling bin, or 'donate to charity' box! These are excellent homes for things you don't like, don't want, or don't use.

Examples of homes:

- Your bathrobe lives on the hook on the back of the bedroom door.

- The papers from your last project live in a labeled file in the filing cabinet.
- Old newspapers live in the recycling bin.
- Catalogs live in a basket by the sofa.
- Your calendar lives on a corner of your desk or on the kitchen counter.
- Photos from last summer live in a box on the shelf with your other photos.
- Those pants that don't fit live in the 'donate to charity' bag.
- The 'donate to charity' bag lives in the hall closet.
- Bills-to-pay live in the basket on your desk.
- Junk mail lives in the garbage can – after it's been shredded.

To be organized you must give everything you own a home. These suggestions are the start of getting you thinking about homes.

Four Tips for Finding Good Homes for Your Stuff

Now, let's dive into the details of creating good homes for your stuff. Fortunately this isn't rocket science. Much of it makes perfect sense; likely you've just not considered it before. Remember, you create homes AFTER you've cleared the worst of the clutter. Don't make the mistake of working to create homes for things you'll be getting rid of!

Tip #1: To Find a Good Home Think of How You Will Use Something

When finding homes for their stuff, disorganized people fall into this common trap. They think about WHAT something is instead of HOW they will use it.

To find good homes for your stuff, you must think HOW you will use something instead of WHAT that something is.

Ask HOW – not WHAT. This habit is extremely important. It can make or break your organizing efforts. Really.

When I was a professional organizer, organizing sessions would often go like this: the client would pick something out of a pile of clutter and say, "this is a magazine." At which point I would reply, "Yes, and HOW are you going to use that 17-year-old issue of Newsweek?" At which point the client would most likely realize old magazines live in the recycling bin.

Asking HOW the magazine would be used would help guide the client to figure out what to do with it and where the best home for it would be.

You've got to think about HOW you'll use something before you think about WHAT it is.

Thinking about how you'll use something gives you a better chance of getting rid of things you no longer use.

For things you will use, asking how easily guides you to the best place to put it.

Tip #2: Keep Things Where You Use Them

As a kid, I rarely put my dirty clothes in the hamper; instead they ended up on my bedroom floor.

You see, our dirty clothes hamper was in the bathroom. I got dressed in my bedroom. Since my mom isn't a born-organized person, she had no idea that if my brother and I had any chance of putting our dirty clothes in the hamper, we needed hampers where we got undressed.

When assigning homes to your stuff, avoid long commutes. Life is easier when you keep things where you use them. Why?

- You'll be more likely to put things away when you're done using them.

- You'll avoid distractions if you don't have to wander to another room to get something. Distractions are huge opportunities for making a mess and getting off track.

- You'll save time getting things out when you want to use them.

Some examples of keeping things where you use them:

- A laundry hamper in each bedroom or where ever else your family undresses.

- Cleaning supplies and rags under each bathroom sink.

- A toy basket in the family room to quickly gather up your children's toys and park them in the basket.

- A pen and notepad in the bathroom, by your bed, or wherever inspiration usually strikes so you can focus on writing down your thoughts and great ideas rather than searching for a place to write them. Or worse, think you'll remember them and write them down later.

If you use something in more than one place and it isn't incredibly expensive or large, buy one for each area. The extra money spent up front will pay off in more time, less stress, and less clutter.

For example, I keep often-used office supplies (stapler, scissors, tape, calculator) in our kitchen as well as the in my home office.

Be on the lookout for things that have homes yet are usually found somewhere else – in a place they are commonly used. That's r clue something needs a home in a place closer to where it's typically used. For example, if your scissors live in the desk, but are often on the kitchen counter, you need two pair – one for the desk and one for the kitchen.

Tip #3: Make Stuff You Use the Most the Easiest to Put Away

If you're like most people, you probably don't have enough storage space to make absolutely everything you use easy to put away. Some things will simply have to live in the basement, or the garage, or on the upper-most shelf.

To help you decide what to put where, follow the habit of making **The Things You Use Most the Easiest to Put Away.**

The premise is quite logical, actually. You'll be more likely to put something away if it is easy to do. So you'll have less clutter if the things you use most often are the easiest to put away.

For example, your everyday dishes should be easier to put away than your Thanksgiving turkey platter. Sure, your turkey platter may sit on the counter for a while until you get around to putting it away, but it will cause less clutter overall than if your everyday dishes are sitting out all the time.

Here are some more examples:

- Keep your everyday placemats within easy reach in the kitchen; store your holiday placemats at the back of the linen closet or in a box in the basement.
- Keep your everyday shoes at the front of your closet; store your ski boots in the sports equipment closet.
- Keep the hammer, pliers, and tape measure hanging on the wall of your workbench, and the miter box tucked on a top shelf.

The question to consider when applying this rule is, "how often do I use this?" Make the stuff you use the most the easiest to put away. Stuff you use less can be stored a little further away.

TIP #4: GROUP SIMILAR THINGS TOGETHER

Naturally organized people often use what you could call "the department approach" to organizing. They store their stuff by function; they create departments to keep all the things used for the same purpose in one place.

Since organized people are big fans of the department approach, let's use it.

Here are some examples of how it works:

- Say you don't remember if you have a pirate costume. Well, if you have a costume department, such as a single box where all the family costumes live, it's very easy to find out if there's a pirate costume in the bunch.

- If all the catalogs live in a basket by the sofa, you don't have to think about where to put them when they come in the mail. The result? They are less likely to be left scattered around the living room. When you need a certain catalog, instead of scrambling around hunting for it you simply check in the catalog basket to find what you want. Plus, having the catalogs in one place may make the task of disposing of outdated ones less daunting.

The department approach reduces decisions and makes it easier to find things and put things away. Departments are especially helpful for people with poor memories. You don't have to remember exactly what you have, just where its department is.

KEY QUESTIONS FOR ASSIGNING HOMES

Here are the questions to ask as you consider the items you're keeping:

How will I use this?

Where am I most likely to use it?

Considering how often I use it, is this the *best* home for it?

Do I have *similar* things to keep it with?

Can I make it *easier* to put away?

Can I make putting it away take *fewer* steps?

CASE STUDIES

Let's work through a couple of examples to make it clear how to create homes for your stuff.

Example One: A Computer Software Manual.

- How will I use this?

    o *I'll use it as a reference if I ever have a question about how my software works.*

- Where am I most likely to use it?

    o *At my computer.*

- Considering how often I use it, is this the best home for it?

    o *Not really because I don't use the manual very often. Most questions are answered by the software's help system. So I can really keep it on the shelf in the far corner of my office. I can find it if I need it, but it doesn't take up prime workspace.*

- Do I have similar things to keep it with?

    o *I do have a few other manuals scattered around the office. I know! I can keep all the manuals together*

*on that shelf and create a Software Manual
Department!*

- How can I make it easier to put away?
  - *It makes no difference what order the manuals
    are in. I'll just put them all on the shelf and use a
    bookend so they don't fall over.*

- Can I make putting it away take *fewer* steps?
  - *Putting a manual on a shelf takes one step. It
    doesn't get any easier than that.*

Example Two: Another Computer Software Manual.

- How will I use this?
  - *I'll use it as a reference if I ever have a question
    about how my software works.*

- Where am I most likely to use it?
  - *At my computer.*

- Considering how often I use it, is this the best home for
  it?
  - *Well whadaya know! I'll never use it, because I
    haven't owned that software for three years. I can
    get rid of the manual!*

- Do I have similar things to keep it with?
  - *Gosh golly gee! In this pile there are 12 other
    manuals for software that I don't own anymore.
    They can all go in the recycling bin!*

Do you get my point?

CHAPTER 7 SUMMARY

KEY POINTS TO REMEMBER ABOUT GIVING EVERYTHING A GOOD HOME

- A **home** is a designated place where something you own belongs.

- A **good home** is a designated place that's easy to remember and suits how often you use an item.

- **Four Tips for Finding Good Homes** for Your Stuff
    1. Think How Often You Use the Item.
    2. Keep Things Where You Use Them.
    3. Make Stuff You Use the Most the Easiest to Put Away.
    4. Group Similar Things Together.

- **Key Questions For Assigning Homes** To Your Stuff
    - How will I use this?
    - Where am I most likely to use it?
    - Considering how often I use it, is this the *best* home for it?
    - Do I have similar things to keep with it?
    - Can I make it easier to put away?
    - Can I make putting it away take fewer steps?

Review Questions

1. **Giving Everything a Good Home:**

   a   Is essential to being Effortlessly Organized.

   b   Encourages you to put stuff away because it's easier to do.

   c   Helps you find things more easily when you need them.

   d   All of the above.

2. The first step in any organizing project is to dash to the store and buy lots of storage containers. _____True   _____False

3. List five homes you could create for your stuff:

   1.

   2.

   3.

   4.

   5.

4. It's more important to think how you'll use something rather than what the thing is. _____True   _____False

5. The things you use the most should be the most difficult to put away.

   _____True   _____False

6. Get started! Before moving on to Step 6, spend your ROWing time making good homes for your stuff.

CHAPTER 8

Step Six: Creating Easy Storage

As I said in the previous chapter, creating storage is a close cousin of finding good homes for your stuff. Yet it's different enough that they deserve separate discussions.

Once you decide where your things will live – the best homes you can find – then you get to decide the best way to store them. Our aim here is easy storage.

Just like good homes, easy storage helps you find things and put them away. Here are three simple principles to guide you in your quest for easy storage.

THREE PRINCIPLES FOR CREATING EASY STORAGE

PRINCIPLE #1 – MAKE THINGS EASY TO DO

If something is difficult to do, you'll be less likely to do it, or you won't do it right away.

It isn't rocket science to see that clutter gathers because we leave things out after we've used them. Shoes, papers, dishes, files, the list could go on and on. It's no surprise either that people who are naturally organized put things away when they're finished with them.

How can you increase the chances that you'll put things away? *Make it easy to do.* You want it to be almost as easy for you to put something where it belongs as it is for you to leave it sitting on the counter, the chair, or the floor.

The best thing about making it easy to put things away is that even when you let things slide a bit and the clutter gathers, you'll find it amazingly easy to quickly get things tidy again.

Check out these examples of things that are hard to do:

- If the file drawer won't open easily you certainly won't put the files back in the drawer.
- If you can't get your hand in the file drawer, you won't file your papers.
- If you can't get the closet door open you won't hang up your shirt.
- If you can't find a hanger in your closet, you won't hang up your shirt.
- If you have to walk into another room to reach a hamper you won't put your clothes in it.
- If the bed is hard to make, you won't make it.

Look at where the messes most likely gather and see if you can make it easier to do.

PRINCIPLE #2 – AIM FOR THE FEWEST STEPS

A close relative of Making Things Easy to Do, the idea of Fewest Steps came from my days as a corporate systems analyst.

As a systems analyst, I was often asked to work with departments in our company to help employees work more efficiently. We'd do this by reducing the number of steps it took to complete a task. How fortunate this approach applies just as well to our homes as it does at work!

The trick to Aiming for the Fewest Steps is considering how many steps it takes to put something away or to complete a task and then adjust it so it takes the fewest steps possible.

For example, to put a pen away in a drawer takes four steps:

1   Grab the pen,

2   Open the drawer,

3   Put the pen in,

4   Shut the drawer.

You can reduce the number of steps to two if the pen lives in a cup on top of your desk or counter

1   Grab the pen

2   Put it in the cup.

Two steps instead of four. Which is easier and which are you more likely to do? Which will result in a greater chance of you putting the pen away?

When you Aim for the Fewest Steps, a desk piled with papers and stuff can be straightened out in a matter of minutes. A child's room littered with toys and clothes can be cleaned up in a flash. So even if you aren't a naturally organized person, you can live like one without having to break a sweat.

Storage designed for the fewest steps is often open. It doesn't have lids or doors or drawers to open. Think of bins, hooks, shelves, cups and baskets.

It's the annoying little steps that get in the way.

If you have to put a suitcase away, which are you m do?

- Shove the suitcase on a shelf with others, or

- Take a bigger suitcase down from the shelf, unzip it, shove the smaller suitcase in, zip the large one up again, and place them all back on the shelf.

See the difference? Even if you don't use the suitcase often, make putting it away take as few steps as possible.

Principle #3 – Remember You'll Forget – Label Storage

One of the common complaints people make after they get organized is they can't remember where anything is.

When you've thoughtfully created homes for your stuff following the tips and habits laid out in this book, forgetting ought to not be such a big problem. However, to help your brain and your family get used to where things now live, it's important to get in the habit of labeling everything.

When creating storage you must **remember you'll forget**. Labels help you get used to your new storage or system and they take a large load off your brain of having to remember where everything is.

Your labels don't have to be fancy. If you put old papers in a box, write a quick list on the box of what's there. Use sticky notes or masking tape.

I realize labeling machines are popular and if you enjoy using them go for it. However, if they just add another step in an already challenging task, go for handwritten, easy labels.

Finally, It's Time for Storage Containers

Okay. You've cleared the clutter, found homes and created storage for your stuff. Now it's time to find containers to store your stuff. Yes, you now have my permission to buy storage containers *if you must*.

Before you dash off to the Container Store and load up your credit card, however, you need some handy guidelines.

Places like the Container Store hate me.

Why?

Why I Rarely Recommend Dashing Out to Buy New Storage Containers

1. *Storage ought to be the final step of any organizing project.* Though to many people it's the most alluring. After all, who wants to be home clearing clutter and sorting piles when they could be out shopping for cool storage?

2. *Storage containers often have a short shelf-life.* Organizing systems change. Those bins and boxes you bring home today might not be what you need a few months from now. So besides having wasted money, you've created MORE clutter! Have you ever tried to get rid of storage containers you paid good money for? It's hard to do.

3. *Storage containers can be expensive.* Especially the pretty ones. And, you never need just one so the price adds up.

So before you rush to Wal-Mart or The Container Store, be sure to read the Seven Principles of Storage Containers and the DIY tip at the end.

SEVEN PRINCIPLES OF STORAGE CONTAINERS:

1. Be creative

All kinds of things can become storage containers. Don't limit yourself to plastic tubs and stacking files. Bowls, pots, plates, trays, cups, baskets, vases, boxes, suitcases, and hooks are practical and often more attractive alternatives.

The essential requirement is the shape of the storage container must match the shape or size of what you're storing. In other words, don't use a small basket for large toys or the toys will still end up piled on the floor next to the basket. Other than that, have fun.

2. Look around your house first

As I've mentioned before, some of the best storage comes from using fun, nice items you already have around the house. Look around.

If you're sentimental as I am, this is a great chance to put things with sweet memories to a new use. On my desk, for instance, I have my whiteboard pens in the little cat food dish of my dear kitten who died a few years ago. Pen, pencils, and scissors reside in a pretty mug my brother gave me. A funny pot in the shape of a pig my husband gave me before we were married holds pushpins by my bulletin board.

Sure, I've got my share of practical step racks, bins, magazine holders, and stacking shelves, but when I can use interesting and sentimental storage, I do so. It makes life more attractive and fun.

3. Measure

Before you hit the stores, know the size of the storage container you need. This may sound obvious, but I can't tell you the number of times I've gone container shopping, positive that I'll know the right size bin when I see it, only to arrive home with a bin that's too small or won't fit on the shelf.

Measure the length, width, and height of the stuff you want to store. Write down the measurements, put them in your wallet and take them to the store along with a tape measure. Measure the bins before you buy.

4. Make sure the container is easy to use

Santa was generous this year so we needed to buy more clear, plastic tubs to get our daughter's new toys under control. Bravely, I hit the after-Christmas organizing sales and carefully measured and selected some new tubs of various sizes.

While waiting in the checkout line to pay for my purchases, I tried getting the lids off the tubs. Guess what? I couldn't get the darn lids off! I tugged and struggled to no avail. If I couldn't tug the lids off, no way could our little girl get them off. And if it isn't easy to get the lids off, do you think she'd put her toys away? No way! So I returned all the boxes to their shelves and started again – this time selecting tubs with lids that opened easily.

The storage you use must be easy to open and close and take the fewest steps necessary. We covered the idea of the fewest steps earlier. Go back and peek at it again if you need a refresher. The deal here is to make things easy to put away and get out.

5. Clear is good (most of the time)

For storage bins that are stored behind closet doors or in cupboards, buy clear bins if you can. You'll need fewer labels and will find things more easily.

My exception to this rule applies to places where the storage

containers are always visible. Why? Though you may not r
your brain processes everything it sees. Your subconscious
confused when too much stuff shows.

6. If it shows, be sure it makes you smile

I'm the first one to want to save a dollar – thank my Scottish
ancestry for that. Yet, if you're selecting a storage container you must
look at often, spend a bit more money and get something you enjoy
looking at. We want your home to be a source of positive energy and
joy. Banish ugly storage wherever you can.

7. Beware Cubbies

Cubbies are shelves with lots of little slots in which to cram stuff.
I've found disorganized people, particularly those with ADHD, are
attracted to cubbies. They buy them and carefully set them up only
to find the cubbies soon become out-of-control clutter magnets.

If you are determined to use cubbies, be sure to clearly label each
slot and keep items requiring similar actions in each slot. Be on the
lookout for the cubbies becoming Clutter Magnets and be ready to
ditch the system quickly if it doesn't work for you.

Easy Organizing Tip: Making Inexpensive Storage Containers

If you want a fun, cheap project to create your own storage
containers (versus buying expensive ones) check out this awesome
idea.

Every once in a while I read a really quick and easy organizing tip
and think, "Man, I wish I'd thought that up!"

Marissa, my favorite blogger from www.newdressaday.com shared
this easy organizing tip for making inexpensive storage containers.

Try This Easy Organizing Tip for Creating Inexpensive Storage Containers

1. Round up some shoe boxes – actually any box with a lid will do.

2. Get yourself a can of colorful spray paint. Be bold. Go bright and sassy.

3. Now set out those newspapers in a well-ventilated space. Don't get all ADHD and sloppy on me here. Do it right. Pick a place where the fumes won't cause brain damage and you won't get paint on anything that matters.

4. Paint those shoe boxes and make yourself some bright and cheery, yet inexpensive storage containers.

5. Let 'em dry and voila'! You've got storage for the price of a can of spray paint (and any new shoes you've had to buy so you'd have enough boxes…).

6. Skip this step at your own peril: After you've moved into your new bins LABEL THEM. Your label doesn't have to be fancy. Write on the box if you must. Just make sure it's legible.

Getting organized doesn't have to be expensive or boring. Be creative and have some fun!

Chapter 8 Summary

Key Points to Remember About Creating Easy Storage

- **Three Principles for Creating Easy Storage**
  1. Make Things Easy to Do.
  2. Aim for the Fewest Steps.
  3. Remember You'll Forget – Label That Storage.
- **Seven Principles of Storage Containers**
  1. Be Creative.
  2. Look Around Your House Before You Buy.
  3. Measure.
  4. Make Sure the Container is Easy to Use.
  5. Clear is *Usually* Good.
  6. If it Shows, Be Sure it Makes You Smile.
  7. Beware of Cubbies.

Review Questions

1. If you can't get your hand in the file drawer to put in one more file you should:

   a   Try harder.

   b   Buy another filing cabinet.

   c   Clean out the darn drawer.

2. Aiming for the Fewest Steps helps you straighten up a mess in a flash.

_____True   _____False

3. To be Effortlessly Organized, you want to make sure it is as difficult as possible to put things away. After all, challenges are character building!

_____True   _____False

4. Storage containers should be practical, not pleasant to look at.

_____True   _____False

5. Now you get to create storage for your stuff! Follow the seven principles of storage containers. What are you waiting for? Get going!

Part Four

The Rest of Your Life Being an Organized Person

Chapter 9

Step Seven: Staying Effortlessly Organized for Life

To this point, we've focused on the ideas and actions to guide you in getting organized. By following the program so far, your home is now visibly tidier and you're enjoying a much calmer life.

Before I wrote this book, I set out to discover what disorganized people really wanted to know so I could make Organized for Life truly useful. The best way I knew to do this was to survey the readers of my newsletter, *ADDed Success*. What did most people ask for? They wanted my book to do more than help them *get* organized – they were desperate to learn how to *stay* organized, too.

This section is your road map to keeping you organized. What's the foundation of the road map? Habits, my dear, habits. But you're about to learn more than just habits. You're also about to discover tips and tricks to keep you effortlessly on track. Remember, being Effortlessly Organized is key to transforming into a reformed messy; someone who will stay Organized for Life.

First you must face something: no matter how organized you

eventually become, deep down you remain a disorganized person. As a reformed messy, part of you will always enjoy making a mess. A tiny piece of you always will have things you would rather do than hang up your clothes or sort through magazines. This isn't a failure of your system; it's a fact of your life and who you are.

It's best to deal with this by expecting it up front. I find my incentive to be organized ebbs and flows. Some months I'm on top of it and hit my zones and ROW every day. Other months it's all I can do to keep the basic clutter at bay.

Accept how far you've come. If you've followed our Six Step Plan, your home is now pretty organized. No more dashing about closing doors before company arrives. Your home may never be spotless, but it will be neat enough! And comfortably lived in.

But as I've told you many times before, getting organized isn't enough. You want to stay organized. Here in Step Seven you're about to learn my time-honed recipe for staying organized.

One last word before we get started: I'm not just passing along someone else's recipe. I've experimented with all the 'ingredients' and tested every step.

I promise you I will never ask you to do something I don't do myself! Some of these tips we've talked about in earlier sections of the book, others are brand new. Enjoy the combination of new and familiar ideas.

Dana's Recipe for Staying Organized for Life

Combine:

- Wise use of **Supportive Tools and Ideas**
- A healthy dose of **Helpful Daily Habits**

- **Doing a Little Every Day**

- A dash of **Creative Motivators**

- Your finest **Positive Attitude of Success**

Blend and simmer slowly for the rest of your life.

SUPPORTIVE TOOLS AND IDEAS FOR STAYING ORGANIZED FOR LIFE

THE QUICK CLUTTER ANALYSIS

When facing a reappearing pile of clutter, do a Quick Clutter Analysis. After all, you've worked hard to this point to rid your world of clutter. Similar to a dentist drilling out the last bit of decay, get to the root cause of the mess.

To do a Quick Clutter Analysis, ask these questions while considering the pile:

- Specifically, what is causing the clutter (papers, mail, CDs, toys, shoes, etc.)?

- How will I use it?

- Where does it live?

- What gets in the way of putting it away?

    - Is it too hard to do?

    - Does it have a home?

    - Am I keeping it where I use it?

    - What would make it easier to put away?

TAKE IT TO THE LAST STEP

Okay. It's true confessions time.

When you return home from traveling do you:

    a   Immediately unpack and put everything away?

    b   Toss your packed suitcase on the floor and step over it for weeks?

    c   Do something in between such as unpack the clothes but leave the suitcase on the floor?

Chances are if you were born disorganized you answered b or c.

What do you suppose that's about? I refuse to believe it's because you're lazy. If you were, you wouldn't be reading this book. More likely you don't unpack because you're not clear on the final step of your trip. In my experience, tasks don't get finished when the final step hasn't been clearly thought through.

Clarify the final step, and you'll improve your chances of finishing projects and tasks. Don't waste time thinking through all the detailed steps of a task. Your time is better spent getting clear on the final step so you know what to shoot for; so you'll know when the project is done.

Let's continue with our suitcase example above. If you're like most people, you consider walking in your front door as the final step in a trip. With that mindset, you don't even think about unpacking right away. You're home. The trip is over. It's time to get on with life.

Yet when you're aware the trip doesn't end until you've unpacked and put the suitcase away, you're likely to do it more quickly.

Let's look at some other areas where a fuzzy idea of the final step gets in the way of finishing things:

- **Paying Bills.** Your last step is filing the statements – not dashing to get the envelopes in the mail.

- **Laundry.** Your last step is hanging up the shirts – not hearing the buzzer announcing the clothes are dry.

- **Writing a Report**. Your last step is clearing away the mass of papers you've collected to prepare the report - not handing the report to your boss.

- **Grocery Shopping**. Your last step is stowing the groceries and stashing the empty sacks - not leaving the full shopping bags on the kitchen counter while you get a snack.

Do you see the pattern?

How do you decide when you need to be clearer on a task's final step? Look for places where you've created homes and done all the stuff we've talked about, yet the clutter still collects.

Consider:

- Where does the mess start?

- Is it because you don't go all the way to the task's final step?

If you're clear on the task's final step and still have clutter, it's likely the final step is too hard to do.

When it comes to putting stuff away, messy people naturally take the easy path. So if it's too hard to put your suitcase away, you'll toss it on the floor instead. If you can't open the file drawer, you'll pile papers instead of filing them.

If you don't complete a task because it's too hard to do, then don't try to force it until you've looked at how you can make it easier.

USE WASTED MINUTES

Small bits of wasted time – even 2 to 3-minute increments – add up quickly over the course of a day, week, and year. Fifteen minutes wasted in a day equals more than one productive week wasted per year!

One of my clients, Pat, was troubled by her cluttered desk. Quickly straightening her desk each morning was her plan, but it was hard for her to remember to do. One day, Pat noticed she spent a lot of time each morning waiting for her computer system to start up and then for her Internet connection.

Pat decided to capture those wasted minutes. Instead of staring at her computer screen, Pat started using that time to straighten her desk. She happily reports that by giving that little attention to her desk each day she is winning the battle with clutter.

It's working so well in her office that she's moved the technique to the kitchen. While she waits for her tea water to boil, she uses the wasted minutes to handle the papers that seem to accumulate on the kitchen counter.

How can you use minutes that would otherwise be wasted? Be on the lookout for routine times you spend waiting and then see how you can use that time. While waiting you can:

- Straighten your desk
- Sort the mail
- Sharpen your pencils
- Make a quick phone call
- Plan your day
- Clear the counter
- Put in a load of laundry

Be aware of getting so involved in the wasted minute task that you get pulled totally off track. Use a reminder like the computer beeping or the kettle whistling to pull you back to your original task.

USE CLEAR REMINDERS

Life is easier if you make reminders for everything and anything you have a hard time remembering to do. In other words, remember you'll forget, so make a reminder.

There are different ways to make reminders. Let's talk about the most common. No one way of reminders works for everyone; experiment to see which gives you the best success.

Smart Phone Reminders

In today's tech savvy world, the most common and easiest reminder comes from a smart-phone. You've heard the saying, "There's an app for that." That saying is especially true in the reminder department. Most reminder apps are free, and many smart phones already have one embedded in the software. The greatest part of this technology is that most people rarely leave their phone behind, making it easy to hear the reminders.

With smart-phones comes a complete onslaught of wonderful task management tools. Among them is a handy little app called Due I found in the app store.

Due works by setting reminders for tasks that may be easily forgotten, like ROWing in your ZONE.

Not only can it set a single reminder such as, "Don't forget to mail Grandma's birthday card," but it sets routine reminders too, like "Water the plants" or "Change over the laundry."

It's user-friendly and makes it easy to set reminders to chime one time only, or as frequently as necessary! Be that every month, every week, or even daily, Due won't forget what my ADHD brain might.

Due makes those difficult things to remember (like daily organizing activities and cleaning chores) become second nature.

While Due isn't free, it is the best $1.99 I've spent to keep my life in order.

Computer Reminders

If you frequently use a computer, try using it to remind you to do things. It's actually pretty easy since most computers come with free calendar software you can use for reminders. You can use white boards or lists as well.

Automatic reminder systems can be a blessing for disorganized folks. My iPhone frequently rescues me from being forgetful. Often with a new client, one of the first things we do is set up a reminder system. It's a simple step that makes a huge difference.

One client, Pete, easily remembers meetings so he doesn't set reminders for them. But Pete has created reminders for the personal and work details he often forgets. He says his ADHD has less power when his computer reminds him to do tasks such as pay his bills, take his medication, call his customers, refill his prescription, and prepare his taxes.

Two Must-Remember Rules for Computer or Smart Phone Reminders

1. Don't dismiss a reminder until you've taken the action or added it to your to-do list.

2. If you're in the middle of something when a reminder pops up, 'snooze' it so the reminder reappears at a more convenient time.

Loving Lists

Another type of reminder is the written list. Personally, along with computer reminders, I live by my lists. Some consider their 'to-do' list an enemy; a nag that's never satisfied with what has been nplished. Your list quickly becomes your friend when you use a ᴸoving List. Think of it as your ally for staying on track and getting things done.

Four Must-Remember Rules for Loving Lists

1 **A Loving List is short.** It contains ONLY as much as you can reasonably expect to accomplish in the time you have each day. For most people that means three to five items.

Cramming too many things on the list is why most people struggle with lists. Why just yesterday one of my clients was complaining how keeping lists didn't work for him. It turned out he had 15 to 20 tasks on his list **each day!** He never finished the tasks on his list, got discouraged, and gave up trying. Chaos reigned.

For your list to be a loving friend it must contain ONLY WHAT YOU CAN DO THAT DAY. If you only have five free minutes in your day to accomplish tasks, than make sure your list has only five minutes worth of stuff to do. If you have a pattern of never finishing the tasks on your daily list, you have too many things on it.

2 **You must rewrite your Loving List each day.** Morning or night; pick a time you can consistently stick to for rewriting your list. (Use a computer or phone app reminder to remind you to rewrite your list.)

3 **You must have your Loving List where you can see it often.** If you're on the road a lot, write it on a post-it and stick it to your steering wheel. If the tasks are mostly for around the house, try a white board in a prominent place (we have ours in the kitchen).

Jennifer, one of my first ADHD coaching clients,

discovered the best place for her to write her list was with a white board pen on her bathroom mirror. That was the only place she would consistently see the list. Whatever works for you! Be creative; experiment.

4   **Let your Loving List guide you through your day.** Check your Loving List often. Cross things off as you finish them. Pick the next task and move on.

This is a habit you must develop. Use our Success Failure Process to make the habit stick. I find that when I do tasks other than the ones on my list, I often stray from my intentions and fritter away time on procrastination or unimportant tasks.

Master Lists

Likely you're wondering about the zillion other tasks on your list? The ones you know you can't get done in a day. Of course you must write them down or else you'll forget.

That's why your **Loving List must have a companion Master List**. The Master List is where you write down everything you want to remember to do and every idea you have. As you write your Loving List each day, pick and choose from your Master List.

Your Master List will be long. That's OK. Keep the most important tasks near the top. Rewrite the whole darn thing every once in a while when you get the urge.

PATTERN PLANNING

Pattern Planning is an excellent technique from the popular ADHD book, _Driven to Distraction,_ by Drs. Ned Hallowell and John Ratey. Luckily, Pattern Planning works for everyone – ADHD or not. Where your Loving List handles your daily tasks, Pattern Planning helps you accomplish those things you want to do each and every week.

Actually, this isn't a new idea. My step-grandma used to do this to plan meals – if it was Tuesday, they were having meatloaf.

I learned while reading the Laura Ingles Wilder classic *Little House in the Big Woods* to our daughter, the Ingles Family would sing a little ditty that sounds an awful lot like Pattern Planning to me:

Wash on Monday

Iron on Tuesday

Mend on Wednesday

Churn on Thursday

Clean on Friday

Bake on Saturday

Rest on Sunday

Mrs. Ingles knew exactly what she had to do each day of the week to stay on track. Pattern Planning is one of those forgotten skills households used to depend upon. (By the way, anytime you're feeling sorry for yourself check out *Little House in the Big Woods* to see what life was like in the 1870's! Makes you want to hug your vacuum cleaner and yell "Hurrah, I'm driving the kid to swimming lessons, yet again!")

Okay. Let's get back to the 21st Century! Let's explore how Pattern Planning can work in our busy, modern day lives.

Pattern Planning helps your life run on auto-pilot to some extent. Pattern Plans are like routines for your week. You do the tasks and appointments you intend to accomplish weekly on the same day week after week. Before long your subconscious remembers what to do when and things just happen.

Naturally, you must include your Pattern Planned tasks on your Loving List or you'll soon forget them.

Ideas for Using Pattern Planning

- Write a book (every Friday afternoon for months I've settled in to my favorite coffee house and written like a woman possessed).

- Clean the house

- Visit the grocery store

- Go to the gym for a work out

- Pay the bills and balance the check book

- Change the towels and sheets

- Back up the computer

- Sweep the front porch

I adore Pattern Planning for three reasons. First, you'll have less stress when tasks and chores get done routinely. Second, you'll stay much more organized when routine tasks are attended to. Third, backlogs don't build up when you do things often, so life is more effortless. When you pay your bills every week, you don't have late charges and it only takes a few minutes.

How to set up your Pattern Plan

Follow these steps to easily get started with Pattern Planning:

3. Make a list of all the regular tasks and chores and appointments you intend to accomplish each week.

4. Make a grid of your week. Use a calendar or appointment book if you like.

5. Plug each item on your list into a regular time slot. For example, you may decide you'll clean the house every

Saturday morning for two hours; you'll go to the gym every Tuesday and Thursday night; you'll pay the bills every Wednesday during your lunch hour; and you'll back up the computer first thing every Friday morning.

6. Make automatic computer or phone reminders or write each thing in your calendar making it easier for you to stay on track.

Pattern Planning is a great tool and a huge step toward staying Organized for Life!

BUILD HELPFUL DAILY HABITS

Next you are going to learn about some daily habits you need to make a part of your life if you are going to be Effortlessly Organized.

Okay, I'm going to be tough on you with this one. I understand how hard creating new habits can be. I know what you're going through. I've been there myself and I've worked with many other people who have been there, too.

You have a choice: you can decide right now that you're hopeless and can't put these daily habits into practice and go back to where you were when you started reading this book. Or you can knuckle down, build on what you've learned, fully embrace these habits and make them a way of life.

Remember back to our Success and Failure Process in Chapter 3? In fact, before you read any further please go back for a quick review. We'll be using the Success and Failure Process in this section to firmly implant some new habits in your brain.

Here's what to do as you read this section:

1. Say each habit aloud while picturing the words as if they were playing on a movie screen in your mind.

2. Say the habits again, except this time, add the words "that's success" at the end. For example, "I hang up my towel. That's success."

I find when I'm tired or ready to stray from my determination to be organized, I hear a voice in my head reminding me to stay on track.

Just last night, exhausted and on my way to bed, I noticed the toilet paper roll was down to the last few sheets. I needed to get out a new roll but my inner messy person whined "don't bother, you can do it later."

At which point my determined-to-be-organized side stepped in saying firmly, "Get out a new roll of toilet paper, Dana. It will only take a second. You always handle little things when you notice them." That mental conversation (and yes, I vividly heard the words) helped me stay on course and stick to my intention of staying organized.

The Helpful Daily Habits

Here are the Helpful Daily Habits along with some hints for using them.

Clear off the dining room table

Every day you MUST clear off the dining room table. I can hear some of you groaning as you read this. I know this is hard. Keeping the dining room table clear is a major challenge for disorganized people.

Hopefully, by this point in the book, your table ought to be pretty clear. Now let's keep it that way.

When you think about it, dining room tables are really just one big clutter magnet. Especially when you don't often eat at the table. You walk by, lay something on the table and there it stays. Before you know it, finding the tabletop is an impossible dream.

When you clear your table every day it only takes a second or two. Often you find the same stuff there all the time: the newspapers, mail, papers to file or deal with, kids art projects, stuff to be repaired or put away.

Every day do a Quick Clutter Analysis on the stuff gathering on the table. After a while most of the stuff will be taken care of and your table will be 'self-cleaning'.

If you eat at your table, you MUST completely clear all dishes, place mats, napkins, etc. after each meal. Since you've made these things easy to put away you'll find doing so takes mere seconds.

Helpful Hint: Try setting the table with a tablecloth and nice centerpiece. Some people tell me this encourages them to keep the table cleared off.

Clear clutter magnets

You've already identified your clutter magnets, eliminated and blocked off all you could. Some clutter magnets remain, of course; beckoning you to pile them with stuff.

Every day you must do a quick sweep of the stuff that's gathered and put it away.

Helpful Hint: Visualize neat and make things easy to put away. My nightstand is a bit of a clutter magnet. I've found simply making a small pile of the books I keep up there makes it look much neater.

Toss the newspapers every day

Old newspapers can clutter up the place very quickly. Give the newspaper a home to live in until it's time to toss it (neatly piled of course). Make it part of your evening ritual to drop the paper in the recycling bin.

Helpful Hint: This rule has served my family well: ar wants to save an article from the paper must do so the da was delivered. Remind people who have problems w most information is available on the Internet.

MAKE THE BEDS

Nothing screams disorganized like an unmade bed. I don't care if you're just going to get back into it again that night, seeing your bed unmade undermines your self-respect.

You must make it easy to make the bed. Avoid bedspreads that you have to fold over the top of the pillows. I love comforter covers and pillow shams – just pull it all up, toss on the pillows and away you go. I didn't say you had to make it perfectly, unless the Marine Corps sergeant is coming over for inspection, just make the darn bed good enough.

Helpful Hints:

- Your kids won't make their beds? Tell them spiders crawl into unmade beds to hide (I'm glad my mom didn't think of this one). Or they can't watch TV until their beds are made.

- Make the bed before you get out of it. While lying in bed, simply prop up the pillows, pull up the sheets, blankets and comforter as straight as you can and slip out. Toss on the pillow shams and you're done.

HANDLE THE MAIL EVERY DAY

Mail is up there with newspapers for causing clutter. Oh, I can hear you groaning. Many people have paid me good money to help clear up the piles of mail they've neglected. Unhandled mail is a huge problem for most messy people.

Set up a mail staging area near a large recycling bin and trashcan. When you bring it in, sort it into piles for each person. Toss the obvious junk. Make a home for the bills to be paid or pay them immediately as one of my clients does. Shred personal papers immediately – don't stack them for later.

Helpful Hints:

- If stray pieces of mail pile up do a Quick Clutter Analysis and set up homes or ways of handling it.

- Eliminate junk mail at the source. Remove your name from mailing lists at the Direct Mail Association. For every credit card account, catalog, or magazine you receive, check the privacy policy and tell them not to sell your name to third parties. I've done this and it has greatly reduced the junk mail I receive.

PUT ALL PURSES / BRIEFCASES / BACKPACKS / COATS AWAY WHEN YOU WALK IN THE DOOR

When you and your family walk in the door do the bags, backpacks, briefcases, purses, etc. get dumped by the door and left there? Take a few extra steps and put them where they belong. They do have homes, don't they?

Helpful Hints:

- If it's too hard to put them away, make easy homes – hooks by the door will do.

- Place a 'collection bowl' by the door – an easy and convenient place to drop your keys and other small stuff during that distracted moment when you walk in the house. Kind of like a temporary home – they don't really belong there, but at least you won't be as apt to lose them.

WASH THE DISHES

Piles of dirty dishes are a hallmark of disorganized people. I feel like a nagging aunt here, but you just must clear away the dirty dishes after each meal.

Perhaps it's too hard to do. Ask why! I for one find unloading a dishwasher totally overwhelming. We don't even use our dishwasher. We use one of those sponge dealies that you put soap in the handle and air-dry the dishes in a drainer that fits in one half of the sink. Before the next meal, we empty the drainer. It helps that we've set up the kitchen so what we use the most is very easy to put away.

Helpful Hint: My Aunt Donna Mae used to put the glasses, utensils, pots and pans away before they were completely dry. Oh, I thought she was wonderfully naughty! She insisted they would dry just fine in the cupboard, and she was right! I've been doing this for years and can't see it has caused any problems.

HANG UP YOUR CLOTHES

When you make it easy to do, hanging up your clothes actually only takes a moment more than tossing them on the floor or chair. Try it for 30 days and see what a difference it makes.

Helpful Hints:

- Clear the unworn stuff from your closet, have enough hangers, make sure the door is easy to open. In other words, do what you can to make hanging up your clothes easy to do.

- Can you get away with wearing the same outfit two days in a row? I can since I work at home. Screw a couple of hooks into the wall to hang the clothes you will wear tomorrow.

HANG UP YOUR BATH TOWEL

Is there truly much to say about this? Wet towels on the floor? Ugh! Wet towels on the bed? Gross!

Helpful Hint: Instead of towel racks in the bathroom, how about using hooks instead? You'll be more likely to hang up the towel if you don't have to fold it.

PUT LAUNDRY IN HAMPER

Make it as easy to toss the dirty clothes in the clothes hamper as it is to toss them on the floor.

Helpful Hints:

- Have a hamper where you are most likely to get undressed.
- Use hampers large enough to hold a few days' worth of laundry.
- Make sure your hampers are easy to get into; no lids, tie strings to tug open, hook or clasps to unlash. Your aim is to be able to toss dirty clothes in from across the room.

FOLD LAUNDRY WHEN IT COMES OUT OF THE DRYER

I still struggle with this habit. But I do have a 'one laundry basket' rule. I only allow myself one laundry basket of unfolded clean clothes to sit in the laundry room at a time.

When I first started my organizing business, I had a single-mom client who's bed was piled so high with clean clothes waiting to be folded she had to sleep on the living room sofa. Needless to say, she was demoralized and embarrassed to be in that condition.

Together we folded everything and put it away in the drawers and closet. Getting through the backlog helped. Then we set up a 'one laundry basket' system for her and she found she liked to fold clothes while watching TV after the kids were asleep for the night.

Helpful Hint: Let go of any perfectionism here. If you can get away without folding some things, do so. I never fold my panties – just toss them in my drawer. If you can fold things more quickly yet less beautifully, do so. Remember, a Marine Corps sergeant isn't dropping by for an inspection!

TAKE CARE OF LITTLE THINGS WHEN YOU NOTICE THEM

When you spy something out of place put it away when you notice it.

See a piece of paper on the floor? Pick it up and toss it in the trash. Notice the dirty socks on the bed? Toss them in the hamper.

I'm not talking about a big cleaning event here, just simply taking care of small additions to the mess when you notice them.

Helpful hint: Messy people often don't see the mess. Visualize neat to help you notice the mess.

DO A LITTLE EVERY DAY

To stay Organized for Life, *do a little every day* must become your mantra. A few routines and 15-minutes of ROWing in your zone is really all it takes.

Most people make the mistake of saving all the chores for the weekend. At face value, this sounds like a good idea. Except when the weekend comes you are faced with an overwhelming number of chores and a desire to do anything BUT those chores. Besides, wouldn't you rather spend your weekends doing more fun stuff?

Sure you'll likely save a few chores for Saturday or Sunday, especially if you work outside your home. However, taking small chunks of time during the week means most of your weekend can be dedicated to fun and frolic.

Row in your Zone for 15-minutes every day

Here's what I want you to do: Find 15 minutes each day, and no more than that, to organize or clean in that week's zone. Set your timer. Put on some energizing music. You can do 27-Thing Flings, Row to the Right, or have a more structured plan of what to do each day. I actually flip back and forth between the three, depending upon how I feel. The important thing is you spend 15 minutes each day organizing your zone.

Trust me here. This will make a huge difference in how easily your home stays organized.

Follow Routines

Do you resist routines? I did for years. After all, routines sound so darn rigid and boring. Not so. I've found that when you design your routines to work for you, they become your good friends. **Routines make your life easier.**

How?

Routines are liberating. They allow the little details of life to get done so things don't pile up as much, easing the guilt and nagging sensation over unfinished tasks.

Routines mean you don't have to struggle to remember to do things. Routines help you go into 'automatic mode' by creating consistent patterns in your day-to-day life. You don't have to think about what to do next. Things just get done.

Okay, how do you start putting routines to work in your life? Here are three suggestions:

1. Use routines for the small details of life you often forget to do. Things like taking medications or vitamins, planning your day, changing the dishtowel, sorting your mail, or turning off the computer printer.

2. Use routines to ease the shift from one ﹐
   For instance, my clients respond well t
   for getting up in the morning, going
   work, and leaving work for home.

3. Use routines to do things now that ﹐
   easier later. Think of them as small guno ﹍ ﹐ ﹍
   putting your clothes in the hamper before you climb
   into bed so you don't have to do it in the morning. Or
   thinking about dinner in the morning, so it isn't such an
   ordeal when you get home from work.

HOW TO CREATE ROUTINES

To create a routine, start small with just one or two everyday
things. For example, wash your face then comb your hair. As it
becomes easier and automatic to do those things, add another step
(brush your teeth). One small step in completing a task leads to the
next step and before you know it, the entire chore is done.

For routines to work, you've got to write them down. Make a list
of all the routines you want to follow. Then choose one or two to start
with.

Remember: Start small! Pick just one or two things at first and
add gradually. Post the list where you'll see it.

What problems can you expect when adapting to a routine?

- **"I don't feel like doing it" syndrome.** Watch out for this
  one! When you find yourself saying you just don't feel
  like doing something, strike a bargain with yourself: Say
  you'll just start and do it for a minute and then you can
  stop if you want to. Usually, once you start you can follow
  through.

- **Things get more complicated than they need to be.**

Sound familiar? If you're struggling with following a routine, it may be because your list of items is too long or ambitious. Keep your routines simple.

- What are the results once routines become your friend? Life will run more easily. The little things will get done more often. And you'll get to do other, more interesting things without being burdened down by guilt from all the things that are left undone.

MOTIVATORS TO ENCOURAGE YOU TO STAY ORGANIZED

In the best of all worlds we are able to stay organized because we want to. However sometimes I find adding a few motivators to boost you on your way really helps.

HAVE A PARTY

A large shindig or a small dinner party; either is a great way to set a deadline for getting the house in tiptop shape. My friend Mary has two small children. She finds inviting another mom and her kids over to play and have lunch encourages her to do many things to spruce up the place she wouldn't do otherwise. Smart girl that Mary!

HAVE HOUSE GUESTS (OR A REGULAR VISITOR...)

Similar to having a party, having house guests stay over can spur you into action. Since much of my family lives in other parts of the country, I use this trick to stay in gear. I find I'm much more attentive to the organizing details in the month before our company arrives on our doorstep.

HAVE A HOME RUN

A Home Run is an easy, quick way to whip the hous shape when the clutter has gotten out of control. Home best when you've given your stuff an easy-to-use home. do the organizing foundation work first.

Here's how to have a Home Run: Set a timer and dash around the house to see if you can clear the clutter before the timer dings.

Lively, fun music helps. Children particularly like Home Runs, as it makes cleaning up a game.

Arrange for a Charity to Stop by Your House for a Pick Up

One of our local charities comes through our neighborhood every couple of months to gather excess stuff for those less fortunate. This deadline is a big help in quickly dashing through the house looking for stuff to give away.

Chapter 9 Summary

Key Points to Remember About Staying Effortlessly Organized for Life!

- The **Quick Clutter Analysis**

    - Specifically, what is causing the clutter?

    - Do I like, need, and use the items?

    - How will I use the items?

    - Where do they live?

    - What gets in the way of putting it away?

        ⊙ Is it too hard to do?

        ⊙ Does it have a good home?

        ⊙ Am I keeping it where I use it?

        ⊙ What would make it easier to put away?

- **Take Things to the Last Step** means to make it easier to finish a project or a task you need to be clear of what your final step truly is. If you've created good home and done what we've talked about, yet clutter continues to collect – it's likely you haven't thought through and don't take the task to the final step!

- **Use Wasted Minutes** (routine times you spend waiting) and figure out ways to productively use that time.

- **Use Clear Reminders** to remind you to do the things you often forget to do.

- **Use Loving Lists** – consider your daily list as your friend to keep you on track and get things done. Four Must Remember Rules for Loving List are:

  1. A Loving List is short and contains only as many things as you can reasonably expect to get done that day.

  2. You must rewrite Loving Lists each day.

  3. You must keep your Loving List where you can see it often.

  4. You must let your Loving List guide you through your day.

- Use a **Master List** to keep track of all the things you want to do but won't get to today. It's the companion to your Loving List.

- Use **Pattern Planning** to make easy to remember routines out of things you want to do each and every week.

- **Build These Helpful Daily Habits**:
  - Clear the junk off the dining room table.
  - Clear your clutter magnets.
  - Toss the newspapers.
  - Make the beds.
  - Handle the mail.
  - Put all purses / briefcases / backpacks / coats away when you walk in the door.
  - Wash the dishes after each meal.
  - Hang up your clothes.

- Hang up your bath towel.

- Put the dirty laundry in the hamper.

- Fold the laundry when it comes out of the dryer.

- Take care of little things when you notice them.

- Make 'Do A Little Every Day' Your Mantra.

- Row in your Zone for 15-minutes every day.

- Create and follow Routines for the small details in life you often forget to do. This will ease the shift from one activity to another and doing small chores now will make your life easier later on.

- Motivators to Encourage You to Stay Organized

  - Have a Party

  - Have House Guests

  - Have a 'Home Run' by setting your timer and dashing around the house to see if you can clear the clutter before the timer rings.

  - Arrange for a Charity to Pick-up Stuff from Your House

REVIEW QUESTIONS

1 A Quick Clutter Analysis helps you banish reappearing piles of clutter for good. _____ True _____ False

2 When you Clarify the Final Step of a task, you improve your chances of finishing a task without leaving a pile of clutter. _____ True _____ False

3 List the tasks you need to Get Clearer on the Final Step:

4   What routine times can you devote to **Capturing Waste Minutes** to get things done?

5   A **Loving List** is a long, overwhelming list of everything you ever hope to get done. _____ True _____ False

6   When will you update your Loving List each day and where will you put it so you can see it?

7   List the steps for setting up your **Pattern Plan.** Now, set up your own Pattern Plan.

8   What four **Daily Habits** are you going to do first and how are you going to remember them?

9   What **Routines** will you do each morning? Evening?

10   Which **Motivators** will you use to regularly stay organized?

Chapter 10

The Last Word

People who live Effortlessly Organized lives look pretty much like everyone else. You won't pick them out of a crowd by how they dress or because they wear a pin saying, "Kiss Me! I'm Organized!" But you will notice something special about them. They're calm; relaxed. Surprises don't ruffle them. They're in comfortable control. They don't expect perfection from themselves or others.

They don't struggle to keep the pieces of their life together. Their life seems to run itself, though if you watch closely you'll notice they do spend a small amount of time each day managing the small things to keep them from becoming big things.

If you ask an Effortlessly Organized person how she does it, she'll probably mention something about routines and doing a bit every day. He'll talk about habits or stopping clutter before it starts.

An Effortlessly Organized person won't ask you to remove your shoes before you enter her house. After all, she's too smart to have floors or carpets she'll need to baby. Life's too short for that.

You'll never find an Effortlessly Organized person's house spotless or sanitized. It will be tidy enough. You'll be comfortable there. You can put your feet up, relax, and not worry about disturbing things.

Are you now an Effortlessly Organized person?

I hope you've found this book useful; even life changing. I hope you are reaping the rewards of getting organized so you can stay organized. I *really* hope you have tasted the freedom of controlling your stuff instead of your stuff controlling you.

I invite you to use *Organized for Life* as a road map to achieve a positive, relaxed approach to organizing; as a reference guide to refocus on getting and staying organized if and when your enthusiasm wanes.

To consistently stay on course, you'll have to do some things you find challenging to remember; things you haven't made habits yet. Don't be surprised if it takes a little while to make your new habits automatic. Revisit the book, be patient, enjoy the process and remember always – you have the right to be successful!

I'll close with this wish of what I want for you:

May your life be easier because you're organized,

May your days flow more calmly,

May you be more relaxed and have more time for creativity and fun.

May your relationships be stronger,

May people learn to trust you to do what you say you'll do,

May you, your family, and your friends find your home a welcoming, enjoyable place to be.

May you now, from this day forward, think and act like an Effortlessly Organized person.

To Your Organizing Success,

Dana

 APPENDIX

Resources/Links

Organizing and ADHD Coaching: http://www.danarayburn.com

Organizing for Dummies: http://www.dummies.com

Direct Marketing Association: https://www.dmachoice.org/

FlyLady: http://www.flylady.net/

Clear Your Clutter with Feng Shui: http://www.spaceclearing.com

Driven to Distraction: http://www.drhallowell.com

National Association of Professional Organizers: http://www.napo.net

INDEX

Made in the USA
Las Vegas, NV
11 January 2021